NEVER
THE
GUNNERS 2

Another Ultimate
ARSENAL

QUIZ BOOK

GRAHAM LISTER

The History Press

This book is dedicated to my late, beautiful wife,
Yvonne Lister, the love of my life,
who sometimes must have thought she'd
married Arsenal as well as me.

First published 2017

The History Press
The Mill, Brimscombe Port
Stroud, Gloucestershire, GL5 2QG
www.thehistorypress.co.uk

British Library Cataloguing in Publication Data.
A catalogue record for this book is available from the British Library.

ISBN 978 0 7509 8257 3

Typesetting and origination by The History Press
Printed and bound by CPI Group (UK) Ltd

Contents

Acknowledgements

Special thanks to my children — Alex Lister and Yvette Hanson — who put up with me while I worked on this book; to fellow Gooners John Robinson (who supplied some of the photos) and Emir Avigdor, who know the euphoria and the frustration; Jim Olford, a source of inspiration; Dave Powter, Steve Fisher, Nikki and Mick Pearson, Hilda Stringer and her family; and of course to the late Mick, Eileen, David and Yvonne Lister, without whom …

Introduction

Part of the serious business of being a football fan is knowing your club's history – and Arsenal's is longer and richer than most. Rich enough, in fact, to provide a fertile hunting ground for another 330 questions in this second volume of the *Ultimate Arsenal Quiz Book*.

Although Sky Sports may sometimes convey the impression that football began with the advent of the Premier League, we know differently. Arsenal have been in existence for 130 years, and this book attempts to embrace that span fully, with questions suggested from a thorough trawl through the history of this great club to test your knowledge of some its more arcane events and obscure personalities, as well as some better known ones.

Hopefully you will find it informative and entertaining as well as challenging. Hopefully too it will remind you just why you support the Gunners – or sway you towards them in the unlikely event that you're not already a fan.

Whether you're competing with friends, testing yourself against fellow Gooners, broadening and deepening your Arsenal knowledge or gauging how much you already know about the club, I hope you enjoy the book.

How This Book Works

As with its predecessor, the first *Ultimate Arsenal Quiz Book* (published in 2013), the concept behind this quiz book is a series of themed chapters or rounds, each focused on a particular aspect of Arsenal history. There are eleven questions in each round, corresponding to the number of players in the team.

It is as up to date as any quiz book can strive to be, but events may have overtaken some of the questions – or answers – by the time you read this. If so, I apologise. The cut-off date was 30 November 2016.

I put together each set of questions and answers myself based on my own research, sources and knowledge gleaned and absorbed during a lifetime supporting Arsenal. I believe the answers to be correct, but if any are found to be wrong, the mistakes are mine and I'll admit the errors.

Happy quizzing, and good luck!

Round

1

Recent History

To ease you into things, this opening round focuses on the recent past, so the questions are about events that are hopefully still fresh in the memory. By recent I mean the interval between 2013 – when the first *Ultimate Arsenal Quiz Book* was published – and now. So we're talking about the last three completed seasons, plus the first few months of the 2016/17 campaign. Not too tough if your short-term memory is in gear, although not every question is necessarily straightforward …

1   What were Arsenal's finishing positions in the Premier League in each of the last three completed seasons up to and including 2015/16?

2   Over which six clubs did Arsenal do the double during the 2015/16 season?

3   Olivier Giroud's brilliant headed equaliser late in the game against Manchester United at Old Trafford in November 2016 was important for more than the point it rescued. What significant barrier did it remove?

4   Which Arsenal player was wrongly sent off at Stamford Bridge in March 2014 in a case of mistaken identity?

5   Who were the respective opponents when the following six players opened their Arsenal goal-scoring accounts: (1) Mesut Ozil; (2) Danny Welbeck; (3) Joel Campbell; (4) Hector Bellerin; (5) Granit Xhaka; (6) Lucas Perez?

6   What linked Arsenal's three goal-scorers in the 3–4 defeat by Liverpool on the opening day of the 2016/17 season?

7   When Arsenal beat Reading 2–0 in the 4th Round of the League Cup on 25 October 2016, who was making his first appearance for the club in two and a half years?

8   Who scored Arsenal's 3 goals in their two League matches against Spurs in 2015/16?

9   How many own goals did opponents score for Arsenal in Premier League games during the 2015/16 season?

10 Who scored for Arsenal against Manchester United both home and away in their 2015/16 Premier League meetings?

11 Apart from being the first goal they had ever scored against Arsenal, what other first did Bournemouth's goal from the penalty spot signify in their 3–1 defeat to the Gunners on 27 November 2016?

The Transfer Trail

Transfers ... the player transactions by which the team can be strengthened and refreshed. As fans we often want more transfers, or bigger transfers, or specific transfers that would bring a special talent to the club (or see a not-so-special one depart); but almost every transfer creates a buzz of excitement and expectation, at least initially. So this is a round about some of the deals Arsenal have conducted over the years.

1   Who are the five most expensive signings Arsenal have ever made, based on transfer fees quoted in the *London Evening Standard*'s reports of the respective deals?

2   Which five players fetched the record transfer fees received by Arsenal — again according to contemporary *London Evening Standard* reports?

3   Many people have said they remember exactly what they were doing when they heard that US President John F. Kennedy had been assassinated on 22 November 1963 — but what player transfer involving Arsenal occurred on the same day?

4   Which four players did Arsenal sign on 31 August 2011 (transfer deadline day)?

5   Which Scots joined Arsenal from (1) Preston North End for £8,750 in 1929; (2) Wolverhampton Wanderers for £30,000 in 1958; (3) Dundee for £62,500 in 1963; Hibernian for £150,000 in 1974; (5) Celtic for £650,000 in 1983?

6   On four occasions Arsenal have broken the British record for the highest transfer fee paid to sign a player. Who were the four players concerned?

7   When George Graham signed for Arsenal from Chelsea in October 1966, which Gunner moved to Stamford Bridge as part of the deal?

8   Which two forwards were signed by Arsenal on the same day – 13 January 1995 – for a combined fee of £3.75 million, and what was the record-breaking aspect of one of the transfers?

9   Who is the odd one out among these eight former Arsenal players, and why: Jimmy Rimmer, Brian Kidd, Frank Stapleton, Viv Anderson, Andy Cole, Mikael Silvestre, Robin van Persie and Danny Welbeck?

10 Which two highly influential Arsenal midfielders left the club to join Italian giants Juventus some twenty-five years apart, both winning Serie A's *Scudetto* in their first season with the *Bianconeri*?

11 Whose transfer to Arsenal in February 2009 made him, at the time, the club's most expensive signing – a status he retained for four and a half years?

To the Manor Born

Formed in 1886 by workers at the Royal Arsenal armaments factory, the football club originally called Dial Square was part of the community of Woolwich on the southern bank of the River Thames – a corner of south-east London that was still administratively in Kent. Arsenal played home matches at various venues in nearby Plumstead, including – for twenty years until relocating to Highbury in 1913 – the Manor Ground. This round is about that early period of Arsenal's history and some of the characters who bestrode it.

1   What was the first trophy won by Arsenal in a senior competition?

2   In 1893/94, their first season as a Football League club, Arsenal faced fourteen opponents home and away in a newly expanded Second Division. Which two of those clubs also competed against Arsenal in the Premier League in 2016/17?

3   After Royal Arsenal became a professional club in 1891 and joined the Football League in 1893, some of the workers at the armaments factory who preferred to play as amateurs formed a new team to fill the void. Some who'd played for Arsenal, including Peter Connolly, John McBean and Bobby Buist, joined the new outfit, which became a founder member of the Southern League, but struggled financially and folded by the end of 1896. What was this club's name?

4   What was the first other southern club that Woolwich Arsenal faced in a League match?

5   Who was the first player to make 100 first-team appearances for Arsenal?

6   In Woolwich Arsenal's promotion campaign of 1903/04, their inside-forward trio scored 66 goals between them. Who were the three strikers concerned?

7   Which Woolwich Arsenal player from the Manor Ground era was hailed by Italy's 1934 and 1938 World Cup-winning manager Vittorio Pozzo as 'the most important man in the history of Italian football', and credited with laying the foundations of skilled football coaching in Italy?

8   Whose decisive intervention in May 1910 effectively
     saved financially imperilled Woolwich Arsenal Football
     Club from oblivion – and paved the way for its pivotal
     relocation from Plumstead to north London?

9   Which two stalwart half-backs joined Arsenal in 1902,
     missed just 3 matches between them in the club's
     promotion season, were involved in the ignominious
     relegation campaign of 1912/13 before having their
     Arsenal careers effectively ended by the First World
     War – and have the distinction of being the first players
     to make more than 300 appearances for the Gunners?

10   Arsenal's last season in Plumstead – 1912/13 – remains
     unrivalled as the most dismal in the club's history. They
     finished twentieth and bottom of the First Division and
     were relegated with their worst ever playing record,
     which featured a mere three wins. A major factor in the
     decline was the sale to Aston Villa in summer 1912 of
     the club's biggest star – a player regarded as one of the
     best in the land – to alleviate debts. Who was he?

11   The tragic deaths – twenty years apart – of which two
     Arsenal players both occurred as a direct consequence
     of their commitment to turning out for the team?

Just Managing

They assemble and train the squad, pick the team, decide the tactics, strive to blend talents and temperaments, are praised when things go well on the pitch, and pilloried when they don't. They are the managers, and to date Arsenal have had eighteen, plus caretakers. Some of them shone, a few of them positively dazzled, and some sputtered and went out; they all did their best. This is a round about the gaffers; how will you manage?

1 Who is the only Arsenal manager to have achieved promotion for the club, guiding his team from the Second Division into the top flight?
2 And who has the unwanted distinction of being the only Arsenal manager to experience relegation with the club?

3   Which trophy-winning Arsenal manager had
    also written Arsenal match reports in the press,
    commentated on their matches for the BBC, edited the
    club programme, worked as the club secretary and as a
    board member, and had also been its managing director?

4   Which Liverpudlian, 1903 FA Cup winner and long-
    serving Arsenal employee joined the club's coaching
    staff in 1913 and became *de facto* caretaker manager
    of the first-team for the last two games of the 1914/15
    season and the remainder of the First World War
    before reverting to behind the scenes roles at Highbury
    from April 1919 until 1939?

5   Who was appointed manager of Arsenal just five years
    after collecting a League championship winner's medal
    with the Gunners?

6   Which former Arsenal captain's 23-match stint as the
    club's caretaker-manager culminated in an FA Cup
    quarter-final appearance and another League title
    triumph for the Gunners?

7   Which Arsenal manager was born into a coal-mining
    family as one of eleven children (three of whom played
    professional football), began his managerial career at
    Northampton Town and managed a munitions factory
    in wartime?

8   Who reportedly said to whom: 'I'm going to make this
    the greatest club in the world and I'm going to make you
    the greatest trainer in the game'?

9   Which Arsenal manager gave Jon Sammels, Peter
    Simpson and Peter Storey their League debuts?

10 Which Arsenal manager was born in Aldershot but as
    a player won 24 caps for Scotland, as well as a League
    championship winner's medal?

11 After the team he managed had been beaten by Arsene
    Wenger's in a late-1990s derby, which ex-Gunner said:
    'Arsenal, especially in the first half, were outstanding.
    On the break they were real quality tonight'?

Trivia Pursuit #1

This pot luck round is a random dip into Arsenal-related odds and ends that will test your general knowledge of Gunners trivia.

So Close ...

1 How many times have Arsenal finished as runners-up
   in major competitions (i.e. second in the League and
   beaten finalists in cup finals)?

Roller Coaster

2 What is the most number of places in the League table
   that Arsenal have climbed or fallen from one season to
   the next?

Grow Your Own

3 Which member of the first Arsenal team to contest the
   final of the FA Youth Cup went on to make nearly 500
   first-team appearances and score nearly 150 goals for
   the club?
4 The Arsenal squad that reached the semi-final of the
   FA Youth Cup in 1983/84 contained five future full
   internationals and a forward who would go on to finish
   top goal-scorer for Arsenal in one memorable season.
   Can you name them?

Winning Ways

5   Arsenal hold the record for most consecutive Premier
     League wins; how many matches did the sequence span
     and when was it set?

Sub Subbed

6   Who came on as a substitute for Mark Randall in
     a League Cup tie against Blackburn Rovers on 18
     December 2007, but was himself replaced by Fran
     Merida after being stretchered off with a dislocated
     shoulder?

Out of Africa

7   Gunners Christopher Wreh and Alex Iwobi are the
     cousin and nephew, respectively, of which two iconic
     African superstars?

French Connections

8   Which Frenchman scored in 3 consecutive matches for
     Arsenal in three different competitions in the space of
     ten days during December 1999?

9   Which three Frenchmen were among the fourteen
     players Arsenal used during the 2006 Champions
     League final against Barcelona, and which other three
     Frenchmen collected FA Cup winners' medals when
     Arsenal beat Aston Villa 4–0 at Wembley in 2015?

Can We Play You Every Week?

10   Up to and including 2016/17, Arsenal had played 14
     competitive matches against this particular opponent
     and won the lot, bagging 41 goals in the process. The
     Gunners' complete record was: played 6 won 6 in the
     League, scoring 20 goals and conceding 5; played 4 won
     4 in the FA Cup, scoring 8 and conceding 3; and played
     4 won 4 in the League Cup, scoring 13 and conceding 5.
     Who are the opponents concerned?

Cosmopolitan Gunners

11   Who are the five Swedish players, four Swiss nationals,
     three Poles and three Argentinians who have played for
     the Arsenal first-team during Arsene Wenger's tenure?

Round 6

Cup Kings

Arsenal have a proud history in the FA Cup, for which they've competed in every season it's been staged since 1889–90 (119). No club has won it more often (twelve times) or appeared in more finals (19) or semi-finals (28) than the Gunners. So this round is dedicated to Arsenal's FA Cup exploits, and as some of the questions are a little tricky, take extra-time if you need it ...

1   Against whom did Arsenal (as Royal Arsenal) play their first-ever FA Cup tie, and what was the result?
2   What is Arsenal's (1) biggest home win; (2) biggest away win; (3) heaviest defeat in the FA Cup (including both qualifying rounds and the competition proper)?
3   Who is Arsenal's all-time leading scorer of FA Cup goals?
4   How many times have Arsenal retained the FA Cup?
5   What is Arsenal's longest unbeaten run in the FA Cup – and what is their longest sequence of consecutive victories?

6   Up to 2015/16, Arsenal had reached a joint-record twenty-eight FA Cup semi-finals, actually played 36 matches at this stage, including replays, and faced nineteen different opponents. (1) How many of those opponents can you name? (2) Who have they played against most times in semi-finals, including replays?

7   When was the last time Arsenal were knocked out of the FA Cup at the 3rd Round stage?

8   What is the most number of matches Arsenal have needed in any one tie to get into the next round of the FA Cup?

9   What was unusual about Arsenal's 5th Round tie against Sheffield United in 1998/99?

10 Up to and including the 2015/16 season, Arsenal had played a total of 464 FA Cup matches. Against which team have they played most times in this competition, including replays?

11 In the context of Arsenal's FA Cup history, what is the connection between the following six teams: Manchester United, Leicester City, Sheffield United, Port Vale, West Ham United and Wigan Athletic?

The Chapman-
Allison Era
(1925–39)

Pioneer and visionary on and off the pitch, Herbert Chapman not only guided Arsenal to their first major trophy and first League championship, he left an indelible mark on the club and football as a whole. Regarded as one of the game's most imaginative and innovative figures, and arguably its boldest and most far-sighted manager, Chapman made Arsenal dominant domestically and admired internationally, bequeathing a legacy that his successor, George Allison, maintained and enhanced. This round is about an illustrious period in the club's history that transformed them from also-rans into the world's biggest club by the end of the 1930s.

1   Where was Herbert Chapman born, which three clubs
    did he manage before Arsenal, and where was he buried
    following his untimely death?

2   Under the terms of whose transfer early in the
    Chapman era did Arsenal have to pay the selling club an
    additional £100 for every goal the player scored in his
    first season as a Gunner?

3   Who did Chapman promote to first-team trainer two
    days after the incumbent, George Hardy, unwisely
    encroached into Chapman's domain, exceeding his
    authority by shouting tactical instructions to the
    players during an FA Cup replay against Port Vale at
    Highbury on 2 February 1927, and giving the manager
    the pretext to implement a change he had wanted to
    make for some time?

25

4   Who was surprised to be switched from inside-
    forward to the left wing over Christmas 1929 in
    a tactical masterstroke by Chapman designed to
    optimise the influence of Alex James as the fulcrum of
    the team by giving him an effective outlet on the left
    for his forward passes?

5   When Arsenal won their first League title in record-
    breaking style in 1930/31, who were their closest rivals,
    finishing as runners-up?

6   Who embarked on a club-record run of scoring in
    9 consecutive matches between 24 October and 19
    December 1931?

7   Who did Arsenal thrash 11–1 in an FA Cup 3rd Round
    tie in 1932? (Give yourself a medal if you can name the
    four goal-scorers.)

8   Who were the three young reserves given their chance
    because of the illness or fatigue of regular starters
    Hapgood, Hulme and Lambert, who made their one and
    only first-team appearance for Arsenal in the infamous
    FA Cup 3rd Round defeat by Walsall in 1933 – and what
    was their fate?

9   After Chapman had won his second League championship
    with Arsenal in 1932/33, he told director George Allison
    that the team needed to be rebuilt and strengthened, and
    identified two physically imposing players that he wanted
    to sign but was unable to before his death in January 1934.
    Allison brought both to Highbury later that year, plus
    another – a cultured wing-half – and the trio became title
    winners in 1934/35 and FA Cup winners the following
    season. Who were the three players concerned and from
    which clubs were they signed?

10 The transfer of which Norfolk farmer's son from
    Norwich City for £6,000 in March 1935 (a winger who
    scored twice on his debut at White Hart Lane in a
    6–0 Arsenal victory) was secured by George Allison's
    willingness to outbid Spurs by £250 and interrupt his
    round of golf to complete the deal?

11 Which diminutive forward made an important
    contribution to Arsenal's 1937/38 title triumph by
    scoring 5 goals in the last 3 matches (all wins), and
    7 overall, but was denied a championship winner's
    medal because his 11 appearances were fewer than the
    minimum required by the League to qualify?

Four Four Two

This is not a round about tactical systems but uses a familiar formation as the basis for questions that are themed around four, four and two. So take up your position and tackle the following.

Four

1   Since the start of the 1993/94 season, when squad numbers were introduced in the Premier League, four different players have worn the No. 4 shirt for Arsenal. Can you name them?

2   Who were the four goal-scorers when Arsenal beat Aston Villa 4–0 at Wembley to win the FA Cup for the second successive season – and record-breaking twelfth time overall – in 2014/15?

3   How many times under Arsene Wenger's management have Arsenal finished the season in fourth place in the Premier League table?

4   Which player has scored 4 or more goals in a match more times than any other in Arsenal history?

Four

5   Who scored 4 of Arsenal's 5 goals against Benfica in an Emirates Cup match prior to the 2014/15 season?

6   During his one season as a Gunner, 1994/95, Swedish midfielder Stefan Schwarz scored 4 goals – 2 in the Premier League and 2 in the European Cup Winners' Cup. Who were the four opposing teams?

7   Which four players made their competitive first-team debuts for Arsenal on 20 September 2011 in a Carling League Cup tie at home to Shrewsbury Town which the Gunners won 3–1?

8   From which four Midlands clubs did Arsenal sign the following four players: (1) Alan Sunderland; (2) Jeff Blockley; (3) Don Howe; (4) Viv Anderson?

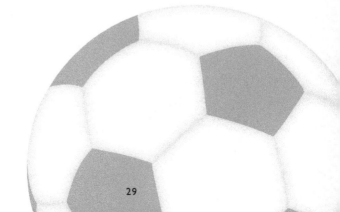

Two

9   Of the 210 different players used by Arsene Wenger in competitive first-team matches for Arsenal up to and including the end of November 2016, two came from the United States of America. Can you name the pair?

10 Which two clubs have played against Arsenal three times in FA Cup finals?

... and a goalie

Every tactical formation lines up in front of a goalkeeper, so to complete the team, the final question in this round concerns a shot-stopper:

11 Since it was first awarded at the end of the 2004/05 season, the Premier League Golden Glove (presented to the goalkeeper with the most clean sheets to his name in Premier League matches that season) has been won by two Arsenal players. Can you name the two keepers concerned?

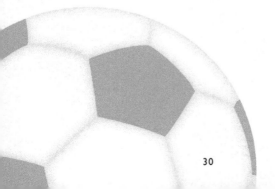

Back of the Net

Goals! They're the lifeblood of football; scoring them is the purpose of the game, and Arsenal had racked up 9,248 across all competitions by the end of November 2016, scored by nearly 500 different players – as well as some unwittingly generous opponents. Every one was cheered by generations of Arsenal fans down the years, so this is a round celebrating some of those goals and the men who put them in the back of the net.

1 How many players have scored 50 or more goals for Arsenal, who is the most recent addition to this exclusive 50+ 'club', and who among the 2016/17 squad is closest to joining it (as at the end of November 2016)?

2 Following their high-profile transfers to Arsenal, how many competitive first-team goals did each of these five star strikers score in his debut season for the club: (1) David Jack; (2) Joe Baker; (3) Malcolm Macdonald; (4) Ian Wright; (5) Alexis Sanchez?

3 Excluding goals scored in penalty shoot-outs, which seven players have scored for Arsenal in European finals?

4 Which full-back was converted to centre-forward in a crisis in November 1922 and responded by scoring 21 goals in the remainder of that season, including 9 in four games over a mere eight days in his new position?

5 Against whom did Alexis Sanchez record his first Arsenal hat-trick, and what record did he set in doing so?

6 Who had scored goals for Arsenal in eleven consecutive seasons up to and including 2016/17?

7 How many goals did Thierry Henry and Robert Pires score between them, across all competitions, in Arsenal's record-breaking 2003/04 campaign?

8 Who scored in each of Arsenal's opening 4 League matches of the following four seasons: 1921/22, 1927/28, 1934/35 and 1946/47?

9 Who has scored most hat-tricks for Arsenal?

10 Whose 29 goals in 1914/15, his debut season as a Gunner, included the first hat-trick scored at Highbury, another treble and two 4-goal hauls, and set a club record for most goals in a season until Jimmy Brain broke it eleven years later?

11 Who was Arsenal's leading goal-scorer in (1) 2011/12; (2) 2012/13; (3) 2013/14; (4) 2014/15; (5) 2015/16?

Round

10

Last Line of Defence

Goalkeeper is football's most specialised position, combining athleticism and agility with alertness and anticipation, sharp reflexes with occasional recklessness, daring and bravery with daftness and the odd blunder. Arsenal have used no fewer than eighty-three goalkeepers to date in competitive first-team matches, and this round is designed to test your knowledge of some of them.

1   Who were the first goalkeepers to appear for Arsenal in (1) an FA Cup tie; (2) their inaugural Football League match; (3) the Football League Cup; and (4) their first-ever appearance in European competition?

2   Which goalkeeper made his Arsenal debut in a 1–0 victory over Liverpool at Anfield – his only first-team appearance that season – and had made 146 appearances for the club before his departure three years later for Aston Villa?

3   Which goalkeeper became the first Arsenal player to win representative honours while at the club?

4   By the end of November 2016, Arsene Wenger had selected seventeen different goalkeepers to start competitive first-team matches during his twenty years at the helm. How many of them can you name?

5   Which goalkeeper signed for Arsenal on three separate occasions in the Edwardian era?

6   Which goalkeeper won an FA Youth Cup winner's medal over a two-legged final against Arsenal, and later collected an FA Cup runners-up medal after keeping goal for the Gunners at Wembley?

7   Although his time with Woolwich Arsenal spanned just thirteen First Division games in 1911/12, this Wales international goalkeeper helped raise the club's profile as one of football's first superstars. A maverick amateur with a playboy image and eccentric playing style, he redefined the goalkeeper's role. He later fought in the First World War and, already decorated for bravery under fire, was killed during the Battle of the Somme in 1916. A century later his death in action was remembered by Arsenal ahead of their match against Tottenham at Emirates Stadium on 6 November 2016. Who is he?

8   Which Arsenal goalkeeper sustained a back injury in an
    international match in 1962 that could not be rectified,
    forcing him to retire a year later when the club staged a
    testimonial for him against Rangers at Highbury?

9   Who served on the Western Front with the Scots
    Guards during the First World War, was a heavyweight
    boxing champion and rugby union captain for his
    brigade, became one of Herbert Chapman's first
    signings when joining Arsenal from Hibernian in 1925
    for a then record fee for a goalkeeper of £4,000, then
    spent three years playing in the USA Soccer League
    before returning to win a League championship medal
    with Arsenal in 1930/31?

10 Who saved a Ruud van Nistelrooy penalty on his
    Arsenal debut and, later, crucially thwarted Juan Roman
    Riquelme and Paul Scholes from the spot?

11 Which three goalkeepers were awarded championship
    winners' medals when Arsenal won the Premier League
    in 2001/02?

Round II

Tom Whittaker at the Helm (1947–56)

Tom Whittaker ranks among Arsenal's most successful managers. His two League titles and one FA Cup matched the trophy haul of Herbert Chapman – the man who promoted him to first-team trainer in the 1920s. Indeed the first trophy Arsenal won without input from Whittaker was the 1970 Fairs Cup. He was regarded with genuine affection by players, staff and fans during nearly four decades of service at Highbury. This round is about Tom and his teams.

1   Having served in the British Army and later the Royal
    Navy during the First World War, Whittaker initially
    worked as an ARP warden in the Second World War
    before becoming an RAF pilot and attaining the rank
    of squadron leader. For what wartime role was he
    awarded the MBE?

2   Returning to Highbury from the RAF, the trainer/physio
    with 'healing hands' became Arsenal's assistant manager
    in 1946 and then, on George Allison's retirement in May
    1947, manager. Which two players did he promptly sign
    to boost a squad that led the table from start to finish in
    1947/48 and secured the Gunners' sixth League title?

3   Who made eight League appearances during 1947/48
    (having made his debut in December 1930), and then
    retired – the last player from the Chapman era to do so?

4   Against which team did Arsenal suffer a shock FA Cup
    3rd Round defeat in January 1948 before completing the
    season as League champions?

5   Who, a couple of months before being signed by
    Arsenal and becoming their inspirational captain, came
    into their dressing room at Goodison Park after
    playing for Everton against them, showed Whittaker
    his damaged knee and sought his advice on treatment –
    prompting a shocked Whittaker to tell his team they'd
    'been playing against only ten men'?

6   Which former RAF PT instructor top-scored with 33
    goals when Arsenal won the title in 1947/48?

7   What (until they repeated the feat in 2014) was unique about Arsenal's ultimately triumphant FA Cup run in 1950?

8   Which winger, signed by Arsenal from Tottenham, scored 5 goals in 4 FA Cup semi-final matches against Chelsea (including two replays) in 1950 and 1952 on his old home ground of White Hart Lane?

9   Who was the slight, ball-playing Scottish inside-forward in Whittaker's team who was hailed in many quarters as 'the second Alex James', and in fact received coaching from James at Highbury?

10 Arsenal's attempt to win the Double in 1951/52 was undermined by a spate of injuries to key players during a punishing period of 10 matches in twenty-nine days late in the season. A makeshift team was thrashed by Manchester United in the championship decider, and the injury jinx persisted in the FA Cup final. (1) Who played against Newcastle United at Wembley despite having, in Whittaker's words, 'a hole in his thigh big enough to put in a small apple'; (2) who broke his wrist three weeks before breaking it again in the final; (3) who twisted his knee after 18 minutes, and was unable to carry on, leaving Arsenal with ten men?

11 In Arsenal's 1952/53 title-winning campaign five forwards between them scored 75 of the team's 96 goals. Who were the prolific quintet?

Spot the Connection #1

In this round, the answers to the first ten questions are the names of former Arsenal players who are linked by a particular distinction. So firstly try to identify each of the players concerned, and then tackle question 11, which asks what it is that connects them.

1   On his arrival at Highbury from Scotland for what at the
    time was regarded as a huge fee, he was immediately
    dubbed 'the new George Best'. Who is he?

2   A native of Ogre, this Baltic defender had won seven
    League titles before becoming a Gunner, but missed out
    on a Premier League champions' medal with Arsenal by
    just 4 matches. Who is he?

3   This Welshman broke into the Arsenal first team on
    the same day that one of the club's greatest captains
    suffered a career-ending broken leg. Who is he?

4   German-born of Spanish descent, this midfielder spent
    loan spells in Greece, Germany and Spain during his
    Arsenal career. Who is he?

5   Following a protracted and acrimonious transfer saga,
    this playmaker went on to make 223 appearances for
    Arsenal, his creativity illuminating an otherwise gloomy
    period in the club's history. Who is he?

6   Named as a defender in the PFA Team of the Season at
    the end of his first campaign as a Gunner, he captained
    Arsenal and has also played for Ajax, Barcelona and
    Roma. Who is he?

7   A PT instructor with the RAF during the war, he
    also played for Crystal Palace and Fulham, and his
    recruitment by Arsenal in his mid-thirties helped spark
    a revival that took the club away from the foot of the
    table. Who is he?

8   This Scandinavian was picked for his country's under-15 handball team before opting to focus on football, and as a Gunner scored in five consecutive victories as Arsenal closed in on a Premier League title. Who is he?

9   An irrepressible Londoner who scored 4 FA Cup final goals during his career, he was regularly top scorer for Arsenal and held the club's all-time goal-scoring record for an eight-year period. Who is he?

10 This musician and World Cup winner was often referred to as 'the invisible wall' in his homeland – a testament to his effectiveness – and had a giant anteater named after him at London Zoo. Who is he?

11 OK, having identified ten players from the above clues, can you work out the particular accomplishment they have in common?

The Wenger Decades (1996–2016)

He is Arsenal's longest serving and most successful manager, now (2016/17) in his twenty-first season with the club to whom he's brought three Premier League titles, six FA Cups, two Doubles, an unbeaten season, a vibrant attacking ethos and some of the most exhilarating football the Gunners have ever played. Despite his achievements — including twenty consecutive top-four finishes and nineteen successive Champions League campaigns — he's been criticised by some disgruntled Arsenal fans seeking change. But many others reject that agenda, especially those with long memories. Proud of their club's loyalty and the manager's ability and commitment, they hope he'll sign another contract. Whenever a successor is appointed, he'll find the club immeasurably stronger and more stable than when Wenger himself took charge, and will have a very solid platform to build on. Whether he'll match the Frenchman's success, style and consistency is a question for the future. For now, though, the questions are about two decades of Arsene's Arsenal.

1   Confirming an open secret in football at the time, who
     said on signing for the Gunners six weeks before their
     new manager was unveiled to the media: 'I'm glad to be
     joining Arsenal and delighted to have the opportunity to
     work with Arsene Wenger'?

2   Up to the end of November 2016, Wenger had selected
     210 different players for the Arsenal first-team during
     twenty years as manager – but can you remember the
     line-up for his first match in charge, against Blackburn
     Rovers at Ewood Park on 12 October 1996?

3   After Wenger won his first north London derby 3–1
     in the teeming rain in November 1996, he described
     beating Tottenham as the best moment of his time at
     Highbury so far. Who scored the Arsenal goals on that
     dramatic afternoon?

4   How many of Arsenal's twelve FA Cup triumphs were
     achieved under Arsene Wenger's management?

5   What unique feat did Wenger achieve in guiding Arsenal
     to the title in 1997/98?

6   What goal-scoring record did Arsenal set when winning
     the title in 2001/02, and what previous club record did
     it break?

7   Since Arsene Wenger was appointed manager of
    Arsenal, London rivals Chelsea have changed their
    manager no fewer than thirteen times. Two men have
    had two stints in charge at Stamford Bridge during this
    period, meaning that a dozen different managers have
    been at the club's disposal (literally) while Wenger
    has been at Arsenal. Can you name those twelve –
    excluding the caretaker stints of Graham Rix, Ray
    Wilkins and Steve Holland?

8   What made Harry Redknapp agree that Arsene Wenger's
    Arsenal was the best team in the world at the time?

9   When Arsenal wore their distinctive red shirts with
    white sleeves for the last time at Highbury, who were
    the visitors, what was the score, what was Dennis
    Bergkamp's contribution and which two players with
    Arsenal connections (one past, one future) were in the
    opposing line-up?

10 What prompted Arsene Wenger to say: 'It was a
    perfect script from a perfectly special player. It showed
    that some things never die like class, motivation and
    desire to win'?

11 What did Arsene Wenger describe as 'The most
    important trophy of my career'?

Seventeen Years of Hurt

After Tom Whittaker's 1952/53 League title, seventeen barren years would elapse before Arsenal lifted a trophy again. Neither Jack Crayston nor George Swindin could reverse the slide into mediocrity, and the longed-for revival also eluded the next manager, the soundtrack to whose tenure was not so much 'Billy Wright, Wright, Wright', more 'Wright must go'. Most of the 1950s and '60s were dismal times for Gooners, made darker by Spurs' success. So this round harks back to a period that really did constitute a drought in Arsenal's fortunes.

1   Arsenal's title defence got off to a shaky start with no
    wins and six defeats in their first eight games of 1953/54,
    culminating in a 7–1 thumping at Sunderland. In what
    position in the Division 1 table did the team ultimately
    finish that season?

2   The arrival of which high-profile former England
    international striker in September 1953 yielded just
    one goal in 9 appearances that season, failing to spark a
    significant upturn?

3   In February 1956, a celebrated coach brought in as
    assistant manager at Arsenal promptly told the playing
    staff that twenty of them would be leaving Highbury
    at the end of the season, and banned players from
    smoking anywhere near the stadium. Within fifty-
    three days he'd left Highbury and returned to Leyton
    Orient. Who was he?

4   What embarrassment did Jack Crayston's team endure
    in January 1958?

5   The 1958/59 League table shows Arsenal had reached
    their highest position since 1953 and until 1971. Where
    did they finish, who was the manager, and what event
    contributed to their 3–0 defeat in an FA Cup 5th Round
    replay at Bramall Lane in the same season?

6   Why was Hillsborough the scene of further FA Cup woe
    for Arsenal in January 1960?

7   The long-awaited arrival of which playmaker at
    Highbury triggered the departure the following day of
    the team's star schemer Jimmy Bloomfield?

8   Why was the 1963/64 season a case of tantalisingly
     near yet frustratingly far, in terms of Arsenal's 'for' and
     'against' columns?

9   One of the undoubted low points of the seventeen-
     year trophy drought was humiliation at the hands of
     Peterborough United in January 1965. The 2–1 FA Cup
     4th Round defeat at the Division 3 club's London Road
     ground was a black day for Gooners but a personal
     triumph for which controversial maverick striker?

10   What decision, unpopular with the majority of fans, was
     taken ahead of the 1965/66 season, designed to herald a
     new dawn for the team and a break from the 'burden' of
     past glories?

11   League and FA Cup defeats by Blackburn Rovers at
     Ewood Park on successive Saturdays in January 1966
     signalled the beginning of the end of Billy Wright's
     managerial reign, and he reacted to the cup exit by
     dropping his two biggest stars. One of them, fans'
     favourite Joe Baker, was sold to Nottingham Forest
     within three weeks. Baker had scored 100 goals for the
     Gunners in 156 appearances, the first against Leyton
     Orient on his debut. Against whom had he scored his
     last Arsenal goal?

London Pride

Arsenal were the first London club to turn professional, the first to join the Football League and the first from the capital to win it. They are also London's most successful club in terms of major honours won (43); Chelsea can claim 26, Tottenham 24, West Ham 5, and the rest – well, very few. Intra-city rivalry is intense; local derbies fierce. This round is about Arsenal's competitive history against, and relationship with, their London rivals.

1   How many London clubs have played derbies against Arsenal in League fixtures?

2   Who were the opponents when Woolwich Arsenal met another London club for the first time in a Football League match?

3   Against whom did Arsenal enjoy their first ever London derby victory in a League match?

4   During the 1978/79 season, Arsenal played six London derbies, winning five, drawing one and scoring 5 goals in a match against each of their three capital rivals. Can you remember the scores of those derbies – and, for a well-earned bonus, the Arsenal scorers?

5   How many of the six Chelsea managers (excluding caretakers) who either played for, coached or managed Arsenal at other times in their careers can you name?

6   It's always particularly satisfying to inflict capital punishment on a London rival, and Arsenal have enjoyed some memorable victories over their metropolitan neighbours. Can you recall the Gunners' biggest wins (all major competitions) against these fellow London clubs: (1) Charlton Athletic; (2) Chelsea; (3) Crystal Palace; (4) QPR; (5) Tottenham Hotspur; (6) West Ham United?

7   October has proved to be a particularly auspicious
     month for Arsenal forwards in terms of scoring hat-
     tricks in London derbies. Who were the marksmen on
     target with trebles in the following derby games: (1)
     Arsenal 5–1 Tottenham, 20 October 1934; (2) Charlton
     1–5 Arsenal, 24 October 1953; (3) Arsenal 5–3 Fulham,
     28 October 1967; (4) Chelsea 2–3 Arsenal, 23 October
     1999; (5) Chelsea 3–5 Arsenal, 29 October 2011?

8   The first eight League meetings between Arsenal and
     Crystal Palace produced 18 goals for the Gunners, and 8
     of them were scored by one player. Who was he?

9   Which former or future Arsenal players won cup finals
     while playing for or managing/coaching the following
     other London clubs in the years specified: (1) West
     Ham in 1964; (2) Spurs 1967; (3) Chelsea 1970; (4)
     Wimbledon 1988; (5) Spurs 1999; (6) Chelsea 2015?

10   Who scored a Highbury hat-trick against West Ham on
     3 March 2001?

11   In League matches on Arsenal's home ground, which
     London rivals have beaten the Gunners (1) only twice in
     a total of 23 meetings; (2) just once in all 16 meetings;
     and (3) never in any of their 27 meetings?

Back With a Bang – Mee and McLintock Restore the Glory

Promoted from physio to manager, Bertie Mee set about building a team captained by Frank McLintock and coached by Don Howe that could finally mount a serious challenge for honours. After two disappointments in League Cup finals, the breakthrough came as the 1970s dawned, with success in Europe and then, spectacularly, on the domestic front. This round is about the challenges and characters, results and rewards of Mee's Arsenal.

1   When the Arsenal board appointed Bertie Mee as successor to Billy Wright a month before England's World Cup triumph in 1966, what safeguard did Mee seek before accepting the job?

2   During his first few months as manager, Mee made three significant additions to the playing squad and one to his coaching staff. Who were the people he brought in?

3   As Mee and Howe began giving some young emerging talents their chance ahead of more experienced players, five senior professionals moved on between August 1969 and July 1970 – to Manchester United, Ipswich Town, Wolves, Hull City and Luton Town, respectively. Who were the five players concerned?

4   Three youngsters graduated from the reserves to make their League debuts in 1969/70, and were firmly in the first-team squad by the time Arsenal met Anderlecht in the Fairs Cup final. Who were they?

5   When Johan Cruyff played against him at Highbury in the Fairs Cup, which Arsenal player's performance prompted the Dutch superstar to suggest that he could become as good as Alfredo di Stefano?

6   What was Arsenal's biggest margin of victory during their 42-match League title-winning campaign of 1970/71?

7   Who was initially a utility player before fitting smoothly into the role of left-sided central defender in Bertie Mee's team, and would surely have earned England recognition had the incumbent in his position not been Bobby Moore?

8   What was unusual about Arsenal's FA Cup campaigns in 1970/71 and 1971/72, which both culminated in Wembley finals?

9   In an era when most teams had a 'hard man', which Arsenal player was famously described as 'the bastards' bastard'?

10 The 1972/73 season saw Arsenal finish runners-up in the League to Bill Shankly's Liverpool, and reach the FA Cup semi-finals for the third consecutive year. What was the result of Arsenal's much-anticipated visit to Anfield that season, and who beat the Gunners in the Hillsborough semi-final?

11 Between signing from Leicester as a midfielder in October 1964 and leaving Highbury (reluctantly and to the dismay of the fans) as a central defender in April 1973, how many appearances did Frank McLintock make for Arsenal?

Round

17

Four Three Three

Time for another round based on a well-known tactical formation, with the questions here themed around fours, threes and threes – plus one to test your goalkeeping knowledge.

Four

1   Which four then current or future Arsenal players won World Cup winners' medals in 1998?

2   Four goals at the start of the 1951/52 season – one in each of the first four games – were among this versatile centre-forward-cum-wing-half's 88 goals as an Arsenal player, before he moved on and set records at two different clubs for scoring most goals in a season. Who is he?

3   Who were the last four players to score 4 goals in a single League match for Arsenal?

4   Which four clubs did Arsenal play, home and away, when attempting to defend the European Fairs Cup in 1970/71?

Three

5   Disappointingly, three members of Arsenal's '100 club' –
    players with a century or more Gunners goals to their
    name – left Arsenal for major rivals Manchester United.
    Who were the trio who swapped north London for Old
    Trafford?

6   Who scored Arsenal's 3 goals when they beat Hull City
    3–2 after extra-time at Wembley in the 2014 FA Cup
    final?

7   Three different players from the same club scored own
    goals in Premier League matches against Arsenal during
    the 2012/13 season. Can you remember the club – and
    the scorers?

Three

8   Three Welshmen have appeared in Arsenal's first team
     during Arsene Wenger's reign; can you name them?

9   Which three former Arsenal players collected Football
     League Division 1 championship winners' medals in the
     last season before the advent of the Premier League,
     missing only five games between them during their
     team's 42-match title triumph?

10   For which three clubs had Mesut Ozil played before he
     signed for Arsenal in 2013?

... and a goalie

Between the posts behind any 4–3–3 formation stands a
goalkeeper, so to complete the team in this round the final
question concerns shot-stoppers.

11   Which three goalkeepers have made most competitive
     first-team appearances for the Gunners – and which
     three have kept most clean sheets?

Round 18

Make Mine a Double

When Arsenal first won the League championship and FA Cup in the same season – the fabled Double – the feat was so rare that they were only the second club to have achieved it in the twentieth century. It has become less elusive in recent years, but Double-winners are still an exclusive club. And the Gunners belong to an even more exclusive section within it, as one of only two clubs to have achieved the Double three times. So it's double points on offer in this round.

1   In each of the three seasons that Arsenal won the Double – 1970/71, 1997/98 and 2001/02 – which teams finished as runners-up to them in (a) the League; (b) the FA Cup?

2   What was unprecedented about their third Double in 2001/02?

3   Cup replays and a European campaign contributed to Arsenal's first Double season being something of a marathon. How many matches did they play throughout 1970/71?

4   Four players reached double figures for goals scored in League and FA Cup when Arsenal won the Double in 1970/71, three in 1997/98, and five in 2001/02. Who were they?

5   During Arsenal's second Double-winning season, an unbeaten 12-match start to the League programme was followed by a run of four defeats in six games between 1 November and 13 December 1997, culminating in a clear-the-air team meeting that was seen as a turning-point, as they didn't lose again until May 1998, by which time they were already League champions. Against whom was the critical home defeat on 13 December that sparked the surge to the title?

6   What was unprecedented about Dennis Bergkamp's hat-trick against Leicester City in Arsenal's 3–3 draw at Filbert Street on 27 August 1997?

7   What was Arsenal's biggest League victory during their 1997/98 Double-winning season?

8 How many replays were Arsenal involved in during their Double-clinching FA Cup run of 1997/98?

9 An Arsenal player was voted *Footballer of the Year* by the Football Writers' Association at the end of each of the Gunners' three Double-winning campaigns. Who were they?

10 How many of the twenty-two players who won Premier League championship medals in 2001/02 (i.e. appeared in at least 10 matches) can you name?

11 The Double has been won eleven times in English football, by seven different clubs. Arsenal share the record for most Doubles with Manchester United (three each), but what two other Double records do Arsenal alone hold?

Terry Neill's Red and White (and Green) Army

Towards the end of the 1970s, now managed by former player Terry Neill and with Don Howe back as coach, Arsenal re-emerged as a renowned cup team – a team with the potential to win the League too, if it hadn't broken up when about to reach its peak. It included six outstanding Irishmen, the greatest of whom was the elegantly and endlessly inventive Liam Brady. This round is about that 1977–80 period of Arsenal's history and some of the players involved.

1   Liam Brady was the creative conductor of Terry Neill's team, but he had been given his debut at the age of 17 by Neill's predecessor Bertie Mee. When and against whom did Brady make his first Arsenal appearance?

2   How many appearances did Brady make for Arsenal in total, and how many goals did he score?

3   Which match – that injury prevented him from completing – did Brady regard as the biggest disappointment of his playing career at Arsenal?

4   Arsenal set a club record for the most FA Cup matches played in a single season when they won the cup in 1979 – then matched that record in reaching the final the following year. How many FA Cup games did they play in each of those two seasons? For a bonus, can you name the opponents in each cup run?

5   Who were the six Irishmen who featured in every one of the four cup finals contested by Terry Neill's team between 1978 and 1980 (three FA Cup, one European Cup Winners' Cup) – and who was a seventh Irishman who appeared in one of them?

6   Neill signed three players from Spurs who played for Arsenal in the 1979 FA Cup victory over Manchester United. Who were they?

7   When David Price supplied the assist for Arsenal's opening goal against Manchester United in the 1979 FA Cup final, two players appeared to connect with the ball simultaneously and hammer it into the net. Who were the two players, and which one was officially credited with the goal?

8 £333,333 striker Malcolm Macdonald missed virtually all of 1978/79 with a serious knee injury, returning for the last match of the season two days after the Gunners' FA Cup triumph. It was his final competitive Arsenal appearance before injury-enforced retirement, and the goal he scored was the last of his 57 for the club. Who were the opponents and what was the score?

9 Who was condemned so unreservedly by the media as a cynical hatchet man that it seemed he'd suddenly and single-handedly invented the professional foul when he tripped Paul Allen in the 1980 FA Cup final?

10 Arsenal's 1980 European Cup Winners' Cup final against Valencia was a bitter experience for the players and fans: (1) In which infamous stadium was it staged; (2) who was Valencia's manager; (3) apart from the fact that Arsenal heartbreakingly lost it, what was significant about the penalty shoot-out that decided the final?

11 The 1979/80 season promised much, but Arsenal ended it empty-handed, primarily because of a punishing schedule. In forty-eight days from 2 April to 19 May 1980, how many matches were the Gunners required to play?

Round
20

Trivia Pursuit #2

Here's more pot luck with another random dip into Gunners-related odds and ends designed to test the depth and breadth of your Arsenal knowledge.

First and Last

1   When Arsenal beat Chelsea 3–0 at Stamford Bridge on 5 April 1997 during Arsene Wenger's first season as manager, a double substitution saw one player coming on for his first appearance under Wenger – but his sixtieth and last as a Gunner – while another was making his first appearance for the club. Who were the two players concerned?

2   Who, on his Arsenal debut, scored the goal that proved to be both the first and last of his ninety-game spell as a Gunner, before a move to London rivals launched him on a colourful managerial career?

Scot-Free

3   Although Scotland has provided many notable characters
     in Arsenal's history, the Gunners have not included a
     Scottish player in their first team for almost twenty years.
     Who was the last Scot to appear for the club?

X Factor

4 Which three players who won full England caps while on Arsenal's books have the letter 'x' in their surnames?

Book Club

5 The following eleven books were written by or about which Arsenal players: (1) *Stillness and Speed*; (2) *Over the Bar*; (3) *Addicted*; (4) *Football Ambassador*; (5) *True Grit*; (6) *True Storey*; (7) *Rock Bottom*; (8) *Forward, Arsenal!* (9) *The Glory and the Grief*; (10) *In the Shadow of a Giant*; (11) *Double Champions: Playing the Arsenal Way*?

Family Affair

6 What are the first names of the following pairs of brothers, all of whom played in competitive matches for the Arsenal first-team: (1) Buist; (2) Compton; (3) Clapton; (4) Hoyte; (5) Black?

S Club 7

7. From which 'S' clubs did Arsenal sign the following players: (1) Charles Buchan; (2) Ted Drake; (3) Mel Charles; (4) Lee Chapman; (5) Brian Marwood; (6) David Platt; (7) José Antonio Reyes?

Utility Man

8 Whose versatility was such that, during an Arsenal career spanning more than 350 appearances (including two FA Cup finals), he was selected in every one of the ten outfield positions, captained the team and also filled in as an emergency goalkeeper on occasion?

3-2-1

9 Of the 841 players who had appeared in competitive first-team matches for Arsenal up to the end of November 2016, only three had surnames beginning with the letter I, only two with the letter U, and just one with the letter Z. Can you identify the players concerned?

Double-Barrelled

10 Five players who have appeared in the Arsenal first-team have double-barrelled surnames. Can you name them?

a.k.a.

11 Which eleven Arsenal players had the following nicknames: (1) Baldie; (2) Snouty; (3) Big 'Ead; (4) Doughy; (5) Flint; (6) Rocky; (7) Tiger; (8) Stan; (9) Stroller; (10) Geordie; (11) Titi?

Title Triumphs

Finishing top of the pile after a gruelling nine-month season of 38 or 42 matches is the ultimate endorsement of a team's credentials, and the Gunners have won England's top tier League title thirteen times. Only Manchester United and Liverpool have won more. Arsenal's next is overdue, but meanwhile here's a round about those they've already claimed.

1   Apart from the 2003/04 'Invincible' season, when they didn't lose a single match, what is the fewest number of defeats Arsenal have suffered during a League title-winning campaign – and what is the most defeats they recorded while winning the League?

2   Arsenal's record points haul is 90, achieved when winning the title in 2003/04. However, if 3 points for a win had been the rule prior to 1981/82 as well as since then, what would have been Arsenal's most productive title triumph in terms of points accrued?

3   When Arsenal won the title for the first time, in 1930/31, two players scored more than 30 League goals apiece, and another was ever-present for all 42 matches. Who were the players concerned?

4   Arsenal kicked off their 1947/48 title-winning season with a run of how many consecutive victories?

5   Arsenal have concluded some of their title-winning campaigns with emphatic victories in the final game: 5–0 in 1930/31 and 1937/38; 8–0 in 1947/48; 6–1 in 1990/91. Can you name the hapless opponents in each case?

6   When securing the title in 1970/71, Arsenal achieved a club record twenty-nine wins, and beat nine teams both home and away. Who were the clubs over whom the Gunners did the double that season?

7   Which eleven players won League championship medals in both the 1988/89 and 1990/91 title-winning seasons?

8   In terms of number of goals conceded, what title-winning season yielded the meanest defensive record – and which one was the least watertight?

9   Who scored Arsenal's first and last goals, respectively, in each of the following League title-winning campaigns: (1) 1970/71; (2) 1988/89; (3) 1990/91; (4) 1997/98; (5) 2001/02; (6) 2003/04?

10 When Arsenal won the League in 1932/33, their two wingers – Cliff Bastin and Joe Hulme – missed just 2 matches between them, and were first and third top scorers, respectively. How many League goals did the pair score between them that season?

11 After the epic title-clinching 2–0 win at Anfield on 26 May 1989, about which Arsenal player did one of Liverpool's say that if a cannonball had been fired at him that day, he would still have controlled it and laid it off to one of the midfielders without a second thought?

It's Happened Again ...

So sang jubilant Arsenal fans on the final day of the 2015/16 season as news filtered through that Spurs were being thumped 5–1 by relegated Newcastle while the Gunners were beating Aston Villa 4–0 at the Emirates. The two results meant Arsenal would again finish above their north London neighbours, and Gooners' euphoria reflected the depth of the rivalry between the clubs, which has been intense and often bitter since Arsenal crossed the Thames and made Islington their home. This is a round about that Arsenal–Spurs rivalry.

1   When, and with what outcome, was the first League meeting between Arsenal and Tottenham?

2   When did Arsenal v Spurs become indisputably a north London derby for the first time?

3   Who headed the winning goal for Arsenal against Tottenham on his debut, and became the first player to score 100 goals for Arsenal before making the short move to White Hart Lane towards the end of his career – a few months after gaining a League championship winners' medal with Arsenal?

4   Who are Arsenal's leading goal-scorers against Spurs across all competitions? (Clue: three players are tied on 8 goals apiece, with two on 7 and two on 6.)

5   Apart from the fact that it was played at Finsbury Park, what was unusual about a summertime victory for Arsenal against Tottenham Hotspur on 29 July 1973?

6   Who resumed his Arsenal career by coming on as a substitute against Spurs in September 2013 – five years after his last Gunners' appearance?

7   Arsenal won all three of the north London derbies they played against Spurs during the 2013/14 season, scoring 4 goals and conceding none. Who netted the Gunners' goals in those matches?

8   Who scored for Arsenal in five successive visits to White Hart Lane?

9   Arsene Wenger boasts an impressive record in north
    London derbies since his arrival at Highbury in 1996,
    pitting his wits against Spurs on forty-nine occasions in
    all competitions by the end of November 2016, winning
    twenty-two of them, drawing twenty and losing seven.
    During those twenty years, Spurs have had no fewer
    than twelve managers (excluding caretakers other than
    David Pleat, who was in 'temporary' charge at White
    Hart Lane for virtually the entire 2003/04 season).
    However, only eleven of them came up against Wenger.
    Who was the lucky Tottenham boss who avoided a
    possible humbling at the hands of Le Boss?

10 Martin Jol's first game as full-time Spurs manager was
    at home to Arsenal on 13 November 2004 – and
    the Gunners won 5–4, in a match that featured nine
    different scorers. Can you remember who scored
    Arsenal's 5?

11 Arsenal have played Spurs a total of nineteen times in
    FA Cup and League Cup matches; how many of those
    games have the Gunners won?

Graham's Silver-Lined Reign (1986–95)

George Graham's appointment as manager in 1986 heralded a purple patch of six major trophies in eight seasons, including a first League title since the Double triumph of 1970/71 in which Graham himself had starred as an elegant midfielder. League champions in 1989 and 1991, the Gunners then became formidable cup fighters, reaching four finals in three consecutive seasons and winning three of them – although by the last of those finals Graham had gone, his reign ended in ignominy following financial scandal. This round is about George's teams and triumphs as Arsenal boss.

1   Who did George Graham sell within weeks of becoming Arsenal manager, then buy back six years later for ten times the price?

2   Who was Graham's first signing for Arsenal?

3   Arsenal won the Littlewoods League Cup in George's first season as manager, but can you remember (1) who they beat in the Wembley final; (2) who scored the goals; (3) who captained the Gunners that day; (4) which two players came on as substitutes in the final; and (5) who had made his first-team debut in the semi-final against Spurs?

4   Against which team did Arsenal achieve an away win on the opening day of both of Graham's League title-winning seasons as Arsenal manager?

5   When Arsenal unforgettably beat Liverpool at Anfield to become 1988/89 League champions, they pipped the Reds to the title by virtue of having scored more goals, as the teams were level on points and goal difference. Every goal scored during the Gunners' campaign thus proved to be gold dust – and five players each contributed 1 goal apiece during the course of the season. Can you name them?

6   The Gunners' title-clinching 2–0 victory over Kenny Dalglish's defending champions and new FA Cup holders defied the odds and immediately entered football folklore, but how many times during that 1988/89 season did Arsenal and Liverpool play each other?

7   Which three players did George Graham sign, each
     for £1 million or more, in the summer of 1990 to
     strengthen his squad for the upcoming 1990/91 League
     campaign, which ended with the Gunners crowned
     champions and the trio picking up medals?

8   What two potentially disastrous blows in autumn 1990
     did Arsenal take in their stride, shrugging them off to
     clinch the League championship in style in May?

9   In terms of tactics, what game is widely considered to
     have been a turning point in George Graham's tenure
     as Arsenal manager, after which greater emphasis was
     placed on tight defence and getting the ball forward
     quickly to recently signed striker Ian Wright?

10   In 1992/93, Arsenal met Sheffield Wednesday in a
     League game at Hillsborough nine days before meeting
     them at Wembley in the FA Cup final – but only one
     player started both the League game and the Cup
     final for Arsenal: (1) who was he; (2) how many of
     the twenty-three Arsenal players used in those two
     matches can you name?

11   In the afterglow of Arsenal's victory over Parma in the
     Cup Winners' Cup final in Copenhagen, which of his
     midfielders did George Graham describe as the club's
     most gifted?

Spot the
Connection #2

This is another of those connection rounds in which the
answers to the first ten questions are former Arsenal players
who all share a particular distinction. So firstly identify the ten
players concerned, and then see if you can spot what it is they
have in common. Good luck.

I   A Scottish striker with a reputation as a rebel, his
     nomadic career included rejection by Clyde because
     of a fiery temper, and suspension by Tottenham after a
     bust-up with a team-mate, prompting him to join rivals
     Woolwich Arsenal, where he averaged a goal every
     three games before financial pressures forced his sale to
     Aston Villa after just two seasons. Who is he?

2   Barry-born, he won 15 caps for Wales, played in each
     of Arsenal's first three FA Cup finals, won three League
     championship medals and had made most appearances
     for the club until his record was overtaken in the 1970s.
     Who is he?

3   A record-breaking transfer brought this stylish England
     international forward and First World War sailor
     to Arsenal, where he added a third FA Cup winner's
     medal to his collection, as well as League championship
     honours, before managing Southend United and
     Middlesbrough. Who is he?

4   After a troubled start as a Gunner, plagued by
     residual injuries from Second Division football that
     physiotherapist Tom Whittaker helped to heal, he
     revealed his true brilliance and became a genuine legend
     – 'one of the all-time greats' according to Matt Busby –
     with the vision and skill to open up the tightest defences.
     Who is he?

5   A centre-half who was very comfortable with the ball at
     his feet, he played an FA Cup final for Arsenal with his
     arm in plaster after breaking it three weeks earlier, and
     the following season won a League championship medal
     before leaving Highbury for the North-East following a
     disagreement over playing styles. Who is he?

6   Undergoing three knee operations in three years,
     injuries blighted the Arsenal career of a player who had
     cost what at the time was a record fee between British
     clubs, who was equally at home in the half-back line or
     spearheading the attack, and who – like his brother –
     captained his country. Who is he?

7   Signed by former Arsenal players Mercer and Docherty
     earlier in his career, he became a Gunner after moving
     across London as a striker, but it was as an elegant
     midfield player that he flourished and won major
     honours at Highbury – later moving into an office there
     and adorning it with more silverware. Who is he?

8   An iconic figure in Arsenal folklore, he defined the term
     'one of our own', cornering the market for attitude,
     sublime and outrageous talent and crucial match-
     winning goals in the early '70s. Who is he?

9   His arrival at Highbury rather than Anfield or Old
     Trafford excited Gooners and the media alike, and
     although never quite as prolific at Arsenal as he'd been
     north of the border, his flair and charisma endeared him
     to the North Bank. Who is he?

10   As a 21 year old, this Londoner scored probably
     the most celebrated, arguably the most famous and
     unquestionably the most dramatic goal in Arsenal's long,
     rich history. Who is he?

11   Having worked out the identities of the ten players
     concerned from the clues given above, can you spot the
     connection between them all?

Round

25

Invincible! The 2003/04 Season

Arsenal achieved something unprecedented in the modern game when they completed an entire 38-match League programme undefeated, a feat previously considered impossible that has not been emulated since. Their exhilarating brand of high-speed attacking football added dazzling lustre to the feat, which was recognised when they were presented with a commemorative gold edition of the Premier League trophy after lifting the full-size silver version as 2003/04 champions. Arsene Wenger's 'Invincibles' eventually extended their unbeaten run to a record 49 matches. Gooners still sing '49, 49 undefeated, playing football the Arsenal Way': it remains one of the proudest and most remarkable achievements in the club's 130-year history. This is a round all about that achievement.

1   Can you name the twenty players who received Premier League championship medals for their unbeaten 2003/04 campaign?

2   What highly controversial match early in the season helped to strengthen team spirit and solidarity?

3   A superb away win in Arsenal's Champions League campaign is regarded by many as a defining moment of their 2003/04 season; who were the opponents, what was the score, and who were the Arsenal scorers?

4   What distinction do these four 'Invincibles' – Sol Campbell, Thierry Henry, Martin Keown and Jens Lehmann – have in common?

5   When Arsenal beat Wolverhampton Wanderers 3–0 at Highbury on Boxing Day 2003, which Wolves player had been a member of the Gunners' triumphant FA Cup final team earlier that year?

6   In both home and away games against Liverpool in 2003/04, Arsenal came from behind to win, picking up 6 vital points. Who scored the Gunners' goals that wiped out Liverpool's 1–0 lead in the 2–1 victory at Anfield, and whose goals secured a 4–2 win at Highbury in which Arsenal had trailed 1–0 and 2–1?

7   Which one of Arsenal's five substitutes for the home game against Liverpool delivered a motivational speech to his team-mates at half-time because he feared they were in shock and feeling sorry for themselves, having fallen 2–1 behind in the wake of two dispiriting cup exits earlier in the week?

8   Leeds United, who'd won at Highbury towards the end
     of the previous season, faced Arsenal three times in
     2003/04 – twice in the Premier League and once in the
     FA Cup – and were thrashed each time. What were the
     scores in the three games, and which Arsenal player
     faced the Gunners in both League games?

9   Which players were voted Arsenal.com Player of the
     Month in each of the ten months (August 2003 to May
     2004 inclusive) of the 'Invincibles' season?

10   After Chelsea, the nearest challengers, lost at Newcastle
     earlier in the day, Arsenal only needed 1 point from their
     game against Spurs to become champions. They duly
     earned a 2–2 draw at White Hart Lane – but how many
     League games did they still have to negotiate, with the
     title already in the bag, to achieve footballing immortality
     by completing an entire season undefeated? Award
     yourself extra points if you can also name the opponents
     and the scores in those remaining matches.

11   Having completed their 38-match 2003/04 season
     without losing, Arsenal had extended their unbeaten
     run to forty games: (1) who were their opponents
     in the second match of 2004/05 when they equalled
     Nottingham Forest's all-time record for consecutive
     matches without defeat; (2) who were their opponents
     when they set a new record of forty-three games;
     (3) who did they beat when extending the record to
     forty-nine?

The 'WM' Formation

The arrival of Herbert Chapman and Charlie Buchan at Arsenal coincided with a change to the offside law. Encouraged by Chapman, Buchan proposed a tactical response to the change involving the centre-half becoming a third defensive back or 'stopper' with zonal marking responsibilities between the two full-backs, who were pushed wider, and a 'roving' inside-forward playing a more withdrawn role between or just ahead of the wing-halves. Dubbed the 'WM' formation, it was developed and refined by astute player recruitment and became the tactical basis of Arsenal's highly effective counter-attacking style in the 1930s. As a salute, this round is 'WM' themed, with the answers to every question being an Arsenal player or players whose surnames begin with either the letter W or the letter M.

1   (W) His Arsenal career spanned only 22 appearances across all competitions, but included a Premier League winner's medal in 2001/02. Who is he?

2   (M x2) These two Ulstermen formed a full-back partnership for Arsenal in the early 1960s, playing more than 100 games together, and making a combined total of nearly 400 appearances between them. Who are they?

3   (W) A Champions League hat-trick early in his Arsenal career and a crucial FA Cup goal against his former club established this England international forward as a Gunner, although he was also unfortunate with injuries that interrupted his progress. Who is he?

4   (M) Successfully converted from left-half to right-back by Herbert Chapman, this east Londoner gave Arsenal many years of splendid service both on and off the pitch. Who is he?

5   (W) This defender crossed the north London divide and picked up an FA Cup winner's medal with Arsenal before spells with Norwich and West Ham and, subsequently, a long and varied career in coaching as an assistant manager. Who is he?

6   (M x2) Both these legendary leaders held the FA Cup aloft for Arsenal, but also experienced the heartache of Wembley defeat while captaining the Gunners. Who are they?

7   (W x2) Two London-born Arsenal full-backs – one of them a League championship winner – made just over 300 appearances between them, mostly during the 1950s, but only occasionally played together in the same starting XI. Who are they?

8   (M) His first of almost a century of Arsenal goals was scored in a 2–1 victory at Wimbledon, his last came in a 3–1 win at Highbury against Everton nearly ten years later; in between he won League championship, FA Cup, League Cup, European and international honours. Who is he?

9   (W) This striker's goal sealed the victory that clinched a League title for Arsenal. It was one of two championship medals he won as a Gunner – and he was also a title winner in his native land, once before joining Arsenal and for three consecutive seasons after leaving them. Who is he?

10   (M) A Scotland international, this winger signed for Arsenal from Hibernian, made the first of his 112 appearances against Burnley, and three years after that scored the last of his 28 Gunners goals against the club he would join just four days later. Who is he?

As with the earlier formation-themed rounds, this one concludes with a question about goalkeepers – and it's a double challenge spanning two different eras but somewhat similar scenarios.

11 (WM x2) (1) This Scot (W), signed as cover, got his opportunity when a long-term injury to this first-choice keeper (M), an England international of the 1930s, gave him the chance to establish himself and collect an FA Cup winner's medal in the process. Who are the two goalkeepers concerned? (2) Opportunity also knocked for this 'keeper (W), who signed as an amateur and ended his career as a Gunners legend, when Billy Wright dropped the incumbent, another Scot (M), in October 1963 and gave him his Arsenal debut against Nottingham Forest. Again, who are the two goalies concerned?

Round

27

European Adventures

Arsenal have become regular participants in UEFA's Champions League during the last twenty years, having first tasted European competition back in 1963/64. But while qualifying is all well and good, their return to date of two trophies from seven European finals has been disappointing for a club with the Gunners' pedigree and ambition. There remains an unfilled space in the cabinet for the Champions League trophy, the lifting of which is increasingly the requirement of a top European club. Meanwhile, Arsenal have built a substantial record of highs and lows on the continent, and this round is designed to test how much you know about their European adventures.

1 To date, the most competitive European games Arsenal have played in any one season is fifteen. Can you remember what that season was?

2 Mesut Ozil's hat-trick in the 6–0 Champions League Group Stage victory over Ludogorets Razgrad on 19 October 2016 was the ninth by an Arsenal player in European competition. Joe Baker and Geoff Strong scored the club's first two European hat-tricks in the Gunners' first ever European game, an Inter-Cities Fairs Cup tie that produced a 7–1 victory over Staevnet in Denmark in 1963. But do you know who scored the other six hat-tricks in Arsenal's European history?

3 As of December 2016, which club had Arsenal played most matches against in European competition?

4 Which two Turkish clubs did Arsenal face in their 2014/15 Champions League campaign?

5 When Arsenal thrashed Ludogorets Razgrad 6–0 in the third Group match of their 2016/17 Champions League campaign, goals by Theo Walcott and Alex Oxlade-Chamberlain meant it was the first time since a 4–2 victory over Sparta Prague on 25 October 2000 that two English players had scored for the club in a Champions League match. Who were the two English goal-scorers on that previous occasion?

6 Which ex-Gunner scored against Arsenal in both home and away legs of a Champions League Group Stage campaign, received a standing ovation from Gooners at the Emirates and declined to celebrate his goals out of respect for his former club?

7   By the end of the Group Stage of their 2016/17
     Champions League campaign, Arsenal had played a total
     of 277 competitive European games. For how many of
     those had Arsene Wenger been manager?

8   Which country's clubs had Arsenal played most matches
     against up to December 2016?

9   In the early 1990s, three players scored the only goals
     of their Arsenal careers while playing in European ties.
     One was a defender, who scored the solitary goal of
     his 25-match Arsenal career in the European Cup. The
     other two were midfielders: one of them netted once
     in 57 Arsenal appearances, and the other twice in 60,
     with their 3 goals all coming in the Cup Winners' Cup.
     Can you work out the identities of the three players
     concerned?

10   Against clubs from which country do Arsenal have their
     worst record in European competition, in terms of win
     percentage?

11   When Arsenal beat Ludogorets Razgrad 3–2 in Bulgaria
     on 1 November 2016, it was the first time they had
     recovered from 2 goals down to win a Champions
     League match since when, and against whom? For a
     well-earned bonus, who scored Arsenal's goals in the
     2 matches concerned?

1–0 to the Arsenal

Well, 1–0, 2–1, 3–2 and similarly close scorelines from memorable Arsenal victories down the years. Football is a results business, as the saying goes, and this round is all about important matches that the Gunners won by a crucial 1-goal margin against various opponents. How will you score?

1   Whose classic headed goal at the City Ground – where League champions and soon-to-be European champions Nottingham Forest hadn't lost a game for almost two years – gave Arsenal a 1–0 victory that put them into the FA Cup quarter-finals in 1979?

2   In the last three games of their 1986/87 League Cup campaign, what pattern of scoring not only underlined Arsenal's resilience but also provided the title for an iconic Arsenal fanzine of the era?

3   Who scored the only goal in Arsenal's 1930 FA Cup semi-final replay against Hull City at Villa Park?

4   What was the significance of Arsenal's 3–2 victory over
     Burnley at Highbury in 1953?

5   When Arsenal beat Manchester United 1–0 at Old
     Trafford in October 1990, who scored the goal and
     what was an unwanted consequence of the match?

6   Whose dramatic late header secured a 2–1 victory
     for Arsenal over eventual champions Leicester City in
     February 2016?

7   Arguably the best atmosphere at any match so far at
     Emirates Stadium was generated on the night of 16
     February 2011 when Barcelona were back in town and
     Arsenal beat them 2–1 in a thrilling Champions League
     Round of 16 clash. The second leg at Camp Nou would
     become a familiar tale of woe, but who scored the first-
     leg goals in London that had Gooners briefly daring to
     believe?

8   Having comprehensively beaten defending champions
     Liverpool 3–0 at Highbury in December 1990, Arsenal
     travelled to Anfield three months later with the Reds
     their only realistic rivals in a two-horse race for the
     title. The Gunners pulled off a classy and resilient 1–0
     victory and held on to the top spot until they were
     crowned champions at the end of that 1990/91 season.
     Who played a slick one–two with Alan Smith before
     burying the decisive goal for Arsenal?

9   Arsenal had needed 3 matches to get past Leeds United
     in the FA Cup in 1982/83, and 4 to eliminate the same
     opponents in 1990/91, so when they were drawn against
     the Yorkshire Whites again in the 4th Round of the
     1992/93 competition, it was hardly a surprise that the
     teams drew 2–2 at Highbury to set up yet another replay.
     On a muddy February pitch in a tribal atmosphere, a
     thriller unfolded – which the Gunners edged. What was
     the score and who scored Arsenal's goals?

10   The longest-running semi-final saga in FA Cup history
     saw Arsenal and Liverpool locked in a series of 4
     matches in 1980. The tie was eventually decided in the
     third replay when the Gunners won 1–0. Where was it
     played and who scored the crucial goal?

11   There were metaphorical fireworks on 4 November
     1989 when Arsenal beat Norwich City 4–3 in a highly
     combustible Highbury thriller. The entertainment began
     with both sets of players applauding David O'Leary for
     reaching a milestone, and ended with most of them
     fighting in the North Bank goalmouth at the final whistle,
     for which both clubs were later fined. In between, there
     had been goals, fouls and bad-tempered flashpoints.
     (1) What milestone had O'Leary, who scored Arsenal's
     third goal, reached; (2) what was particularly significant
     about Lee Dixon's 2 goals; (3) who scored the first
     Arsenal goal?

Round

29

Finals Fling

Yes, the theme of this round is the numerous cup finals in which the Gunners have participated over the years for various pieces of silverware.

1   How many cup finals have Arsenal reached, in total, throughout their history? (FA Cup, League Cup and European competitions.)
2   How many FA Cup finals have Arsenal won wearing yellow shirts?
3   Who captained Arsenal in their first FA Cup final – and their most recent?
4   And who were the captains for Arsenal's first, and their most recent, European finals?

5   Arsenal fans of various generations have celebrated 43 cup final goals across all competitions, scored by thirty-six different players. Seven of those players have scored 2 cup final goals, and two of those seven got doubles (i.e. 2 goals in I match). Who are the seven and which two were double marksmen?

6   Who was the first player to come on as a substitute for Arsenal in a cup final?

7   What particular distinction do the following ten Arsenal players, past and present, have in common: Viv Anderson, Petr Cech, Lassana Diarra, William Gallas, Sebastian Larsson, Paul Mariner, Emmanuel Petit, Mikael Silvestre, Brian Talbot and Giovani van Bronckhorst?

8   Among other things, Arsenal's FA Cup final triumphs of 1993, 2002 and 2005 were notable for the fact that each marked the last first-team appearance of a Gunners legend. Who were the players concerned?

9   What final feat have these four Gunners all performed: Martin Hayes, Ray Kennedy, Olivier Giroud and Eddie Kelly?

10 Arsenal have suffered the handicap of losing four players to red cards during cup finals. Can you name the inglorious quartet?

11 How many times have Arsenal come from behind to win a cup final?

Round

30

End-Game

And finally – we've reached the last round of questions, so this one is all about last times. Hopefully you've enjoyed the challenges, and the questions have stirred some good memories. So now, for the last time …

1   What was the result of Arsenal's final game at the Manor Ground before they moved north-west to Highbury?

2   What was the last League game Arsenal played outside the top flight (old First Division or Premier League) – and for a bonus, what was the result and who scored the goals?

3   What was significant for Arsenal about the Football League's final table for Division Two at the end of the 1914/15 season?

4   Who were the opponents, what was the score and
    who scored for Arsenal in the club's last League match
    – since removed from the records – before Football
    League and FA Cup football was suspended on the
    outbreak of the Second World War for the duration of
    the hostilities?

5   Following the abandonment of the 1939/40 season,
    Arsenal's last official League match prior to the
    resumption of League football in August 1946 was, by
    default, their final game of the 1938/39 season, a 2–0
    home win over Brentford immortalised on film in *The
    Arsenal Stadium Mystery.* Who scored the Gunners' goals
    in that match and thus had the distinction of being the
    club's last League scorers for over seven years?

6   Against whom did Ian Wright score (1) the last of
    his 185 goals for Arsenal; (2) his last League goal for
    Arsenal; (3) his last goal at Highbury for Arsenal?

7   What was the result of the last competitive first-team
    match that Arsenal played before Arsene Wenger
    officially took over as manager?

8   Who was the last Scotsman to score for Arsenal in a
    competitive first-team fixture – and the last Irishman?

9   In the club's final season at Highbury, Arsenal beat
    Middlesbrough 7–0. Can you recall who scored the
    goals that day (14 January 2006)?

10 When was the last time Arsenal finished a League
    campaign outside of the top six positions?

11 Up to 2015/16, when was the last time Tottenham
    Hotspur finished above Arsenal in the League table?

Recent History

1 The Gunners finished 4th in 2013/14, 3rd in 2014/15 and 2nd in 2015/16.
2 Aston Villa (4–0 at home, 2–0 away); Bournemouth (2–0, 2–0); Everton (2–1, 2–0); Leicester City (2–1, 5–2); Newcastle United (1–0, 1–0); and Watford (4–0, 3–0).
3 It was the first goal Arsenal had scored in the Premier League against a José Mourinho team since May 2007, when Gilberto Silva scored in a 1–1 draw against Chelsea.
4 Kieran Gibbs got the red card when it was Alex Oxlade-Chamberlain who had handled – one more thing that went spectacularly wrong on that miserable day.
5 (1) Napoli; (2) Aston Villa; (3) Swansea City; (4) Aston Villa; (5) Hull City; (6) Nottingham Forest.
6 Theo Walcott, Alex Oxlade-Chamberlain and Calum Chambers had all joined Arsenal from Southampton.
7 Right-back Carl Jenkinson, whose previous first-team appearance for Arsenal had been on 11 May 2014, when he scored in a 2–0 Premier League victory over Norwich City at Carrow Road.
8 Kieran Gibbs in the 1–1 draw at home; Aaron Ramsey and Alexis Sanchez at White Hart Lane.
9 Three: Damien Delaney (Crystal Palace), Fabricio Coloccini (Newcastle Utd), Mark Bunn (Aston Villa).
10 Mesut Ozil.
11 It resulted from the awarding of a penalty against Arsenal in consecutive home games for the first time in the Premier League.

The Transfer Trail

1 (1) Mesut Ozil (£42.5 million) from Real Madrid;
(2) Shkodran Mustafi (£35 million) from Valencia;
(3) Granit Xhaka (£33.8 million) from Borussia
Monchengladbach; (4) Alexis Sanchez (£31.7 million) from
Barcelona; (5) Lucas Perez (£17 million) from Deportivo
La Coruna.

2 (1) Cesc Fabregas (£29.8 million plus £5.3 million in add-
ons) to Barcelona; (2,3) Marc Overmars (£25 million)
to Barcelona and Emmanuel Adebayor (£25 million)
to Manchester City; (4) Samir Nasri (£24 million) to
Manchester City; (5) Nicolas Anelka (£23.5 million) to
Real Madrid.

3 Goalkeeper Jim Furnell joined the Gunners from Liverpool
for £18,000 and made his debut the following day at
Highbury against Blackpool, a match Arsenal won 5–3.

4 Mikel Arteta (from Everton), Per Mertesacker (Werder
Bremen), Andre Santos (Fenerbahce) and Yossi Benayoun
(on loan from Chelsea). Ju Young Park had signed the
previous day.

5 (1) Alex James; (2) Jackie Henderson; (3) Ian Ure; (4) Alex
Cropley; (5) Charlie Nicholas.

6 (1) David Jack from Bolton Wanderers in 1928 for £10,890;
(2) Bryn Jones from Wolves in 1938 for £14,500;
(3) Alan Ball from Everton in 1971 for £220,000;
(4) Dennis Bergkamp from Internazionale in 1995 for
£7,500,000.

7 Tommy Baldwin.

8 In two of his final three transfer deals for Arsenal, George Graham signed John Hartson for £2.5 million from Luton Town and Chris Kiwomya for £1.25 million from Ipswich Town; Hartson was 19 and his transfer fee was a British record for a teenager at the time.

9 Andy Cole – all the others were transferred directly between Arsenal and Manchester United, whereas Cole joined the Red Devils from Newcastle, having been sold by Arsenal to Bristol City.

10 Liam Brady (1980) and Patrick Vieira (2005).

11 Andrey Arshavin, who cost £15 million when transferred from Zenit St Petersburg in February 2009. He remained Arsenal's costliest signing until Mesut Ozil arrived for £42.5 million from Real Madrid on 2 September 2013.

Round 3

To the Manor Born

1 Playing as Royal Arsenal, the club won the Kent Senior Cup on 21 March 1890 when they beat Thanet Wanderers 3–0 at Chatham in the final.

2 Liverpool and Ardwick – who the following season changed their name to Manchester City. For the record, the other Division 2 clubs in 1893/94 were Small Heath (later called Birmingham City), Notts County, Newcastle United, Grimsby Town, Burton Swifts, Burslem Port Vale, Lincoln City, Walsall Town Swifts, Middlesbrough Ironopolis, Crewe Alexandra, Rotherham Town and Northwich Victoria.

3 Royal Ordnance Factories Football Club.

4 Luton Town, in 1897/98.

5 Scottish winger or right-half Gavin Crawford.

6 Tommy Shanks (24 goals), John 'Tim' Coleman (23) and Bill Gooing (19).

7 Bill Garbutt, who joined Arsenal as a young winger in December 1905 and made 65 appearances, scoring 14 goals, before moving to Blackburn Rovers in May 1908. When injury ended his playing career prematurely, he moved to Genoa to work in the docks and was appointed head coach of Genoa in 1912, aged 29 and with no prior coaching experience. Under his guidance, Genoa won the Italian title in 1915, 1923 and 1924 – and haven't won it since. Garbutt also led Athletic Bilbao to the Spanish championship in 1936.

8 Henry Norris, who paid off all Arsenal's debts and pledged to keep them in Plumstead if the local community would provide sufficient support to make the club self-financing.
But as attendances continued to dwindle, Norris implemented his ambitious plan to find Arsenal a more accessible location offering a bigger potential fan-base – Highbury.

9 Roddy McEachrane and Percy Sands. Inverness-born Roddy joined Arsenal from Thames Ironworks (later West Ham United) in May 1902 and made 346 appearances for the club over the next eleven years. The Arsenal career of centre-half Percy Sands, a schoolteacher from Norwood, spanned seventeen seasons. An Arsenal captain, he served in the Royal Army Medical Corps during the First World War, and when he left the club in 1919, had 350 appearances and 12 goals to his name.

10 Andy Ducat, who made 188 appearances for Arsenal, scoring 21 goals, and represented England at both football and cricket.

11 Joe Powell and Bob Benson. Joe broke his arm in a United League match against Kettering Town in November 1896, contracted blood poisoning and tetanus as a result and, despite having the arm amputated, died a week later. He was just 26 and had made 92 appearances for Arsenal, scoring twice. Bob joined Woolwich Arsenal soon after the club's move to Highbury, and made 54 appearances (7 goals) before the First World War – during which he worked at the Royal Arsenal munitions factory. On 19 February 1916 he was at Highbury to watch a London Combination match and when Joe Shaw was unable to play, Bob volunteered to take his place – despite not having played for nearly a year and lacking match fitness. During the game he collapsed, was taken off, and died in the dressing room in trainer George Hardy's arms.

Just Managing

1 Harry Bradshaw, who took Arsenal into the First Division in 1903/04 as Second Division runners-up, a point behind Preston North End – then promptly left to manage Fulham.

2 George Morrell, who had been in charge from 1908 and who survived the drop to lead the Gunners in their first season at Highbury.

3 The multi-talented George Allison, the club's second longest-serving manager after Arsene Wenger.

4 James 'Punch' McEwan, who initially worked under manager George Morrell at Arsenal, but took charge of first-team affairs when Morrell resigned his post. Punch stayed on as caretaker manager until handing over to Leslie Knighton in 1919 and resuming his duties developing the club's younger players, managing the 'A' team under Herbert Chapman and working as a dressing-room attendant before leaving just prior to the outbreak of the Second World War.

5 Goalkeeper George Swindin, who made 14 appearances during Arsenal's seventh League title-winning campaign of 1952/53, and became Arsenal manager in June 1958 after a successful few years managing Peterborough United.

6 Joe Shaw, who took the reins in the immediate aftermath of Herbert Chapman's sudden death in January 1934 and guided Arsenal to a second successive League championship in 1933/34 before reverting to reserve team manager. He later became assistant manager to Tom Whittaker and also worked as an Arsenal club ambassador before retiring in 1956, having served Arsenal for almost fifty years.

7 The incomparable Herbert Chapman.

8 Herbert Chapman said this to Tom Whittaker (the latter recounted) when promoting him to first-team trainer in 1927. Twenty years later Whittaker himself became one of Arsenal's most successful managers.

9 Billy Wright – in 1963 (v Blackpool), 1964 (v Chelsea) and 1965 (v Leicester), respectively.

10 Bruce Rioch. The son of a regimental sergeant major in the Scots Guards, he was in Derby County's title-winning side of 1974/75, and captained Scotland at the 1978 World Cup.

11 Former double-winning Arsenal player and multiple trophy-winning manager George Graham, then in charge at Spurs, following Arsenal's 3–1 victory at White Hart Lane in April 1999.

Trivia Pursuit #1

So Close ...

1 Arsenal have finished as runners-up on twenty-seven occasions overall – ten times in the League (1903–04 in Division 2; 1925–26, 1931–32, 1972–73 in Division 1; 1998–99, 1999–2000, 2000–01, 2002–03, 2004–05 & 2015–16 in the Premier League); seven times in the FA Cup (1927, 1932, 1952, 1972, 1978, 1980 & 2001); five times in the League Cup (1968, 1969, 1988, 2007 & 2011); and five times in European competition (1980 and 1995 Cup Winners' Cup, 1995 Super Cup, 2000 UEFA Cup, 2006 Champions League).

Roller Coaster

2 Eighteen in 1925/26, Herbert Chapman's first season as manager, when they finished second in Division 1, a jump of eighteen places from their twentieth position in 1924/25 (Leslie Knighton's final campaign).

Grow Your Own

3 John Radford (476 appearances plus 6 as a substitute; 149 goals).

4 Tony Adams (66 England caps), Martin Keown (43), Michael Thomas (2), David Rocastle (14), plus Niall Quinn (91 Republic of Ireland caps); Martin Hayes was Arsenal's leading scorer in 1986/87 with 24 goals.

Winning Ways

5 The record is fourteen successive Premier League wins and Arsenal set it with a run that started with a 1–0 victory over Everton (away) on 10 February 2002, and continued until they drew 2–2 at West Ham United on 24 August that year.

Sub Subbed

6 Nacer Barazite.

Out of Africa

7 Liberian former FIFA World Player of the Year George Weah is Chris Wreh's cousin, while Nigeria's two-time BBC African Footballer of the Year Jay-Jay Okocha is Alex Iwobi's uncle.

French Connections

8 Gilles Grimandi, who netted in a 3–0 Premier League win at Leicester on 4 December, a 3–3 draw away to Nantes in the UEFA Cup on 9 December, and a 3–1 FA Cup 3rd Round victory over Blackpool at Highbury on 13 December. (Coincidentally, Marc Overmars also scored in each of those 3 matches.)

9 Robert Pires, Thierry Henry and Mathieu Flamini were the Frenchmen among the fourteen players Arsenal used during the 2006 Champions League final against Barcelona, while Laurent Koscielny, Francis Coquelin and Olivier Giroud were their compatriots who collected FA Cup winners' medals when Arsenal beat Aston Villa 4–0 at Wembley in 2015.

Can We Play You Every Week?

10 Reading are the hapless opponents still awaiting a win, or even a draw, against Arsenal after fourteen attempts across three competitions from February 1935 until October 2016.

Cosmopolitan Gunners

11 Freddie Ljungberg, Rami Shaaban, Sebastian Larsson, Kristoffer Olsson and Kim Kallstrom are the five Swedes; Philippe Senderos, Johan Djourou, Martin Angha and Granit Xhaka are the four Swiss players; Lukasz Fabianski, Wojciech Szczesny and Krystian Bielik are the three Poles; while Fabian Caballero, Nelson Vivas and Emiliano Martinez are the three from Argentina.

Cup Kings

1 Royal Arsenal beat Lyndhurst 11–0 at home (Manor Field, later to be called the Manor Ground) on 5 October 1889 in Round 1 of that season's FA Cup Qualifying Competition.

2 (1) 12–0 v Ashford United in the 1st Qualifying Round, 14 October 1893; (2) 7–1 at Burnley in a 5th Round tie on 20 February 1937; (3) 0–6, which they've suffered three times: away to Sunderland in the 1st Round, 21 January 1893; at home to Derby County in the 1st Round, 28 January 1899; and away to West Ham United on 5 January 1946, in the 3rd Round, 1st leg.

3 Cliff Bastin with 26.

4 Twice – in 2003, after winning it in 2002; and in 2015 after victory in 2014.

5 Twenty-one matches from 6 January 1979 to 1 May 1980; the run included ten draws and ten replays. Arsenal also went 18 matches unbeaten between 5 January 2002 and 6 March 2004 (winning 18); and 16 matches unbeaten from 4 January 2014 until 8 March 2016, winning 15 – a sequence that included their longest-ever run of consecutive FA Cup victories (14).

6 Newcastle United (1906); Sheffield Wednesday (1907);
Southampton (1927); Blackburn Rovers (1928 and 2005);
Hull City (1930); Manchester City (1932); Grimsby Town
(1936); Chelsea (1950, 1952 and 2009); Stoke City (1971
and 1972); Sunderland (1973); Orient (1978); Wolves
(1979 and 1998); Liverpool (1980); Manchester United
(1983, 1999 and 2004); Spurs (1991, 1993 and 2001);
Middlesbrough (2002); Sheffield United (2003); Wigan
Athletic (2014); and Reading (2015). They've played most
semi-final matches against Chelsea (5 including two replays),
followed by Liverpool and Stoke (4 each).

7 In 1995/96 on 17 January 1996 – in a 3rd Round replay at
Sheffield United, when Bruce Rioch was manager.

8 Five in 1978/79 against Sheffield Wednesday in the 3rd
Round.

9 Arsenal won the original tie 2–1 at Highbury, but Arsene
Wenger immediately offered to have the result annulled
and the tie played again because of the perceived
unsporting nature of the winning goal. The match was
played again ten days later. Arsenal won that one 2–1, too.

10 Arsenal have played 19 FA Cup matches against Chelsea
(won 8, drawn 6, lost 5). Next on the list come Liverpool
(17), Leeds United (16), West Ham United (15) and
Manchester United (15).

11 They all had FA Cup ties against Arsenal resolved by a
penalty shoot-out.

The Chapman–Allison Era (1925–39)

1 Chapman was born at Kiveton Park near Sheffield in Yorkshire. He managed Northampton Town, Leeds City and Huddersfield Town before Arsenal. He is buried in the churchyard of St Mary's Church, Hendon.

2 Charlie Buchan, Herbert Chapman's first signing as Arsenal manager in July 1925. Club chairman Sir Henry Norris proposed a compromise regarding Sunderland's asking price of £4,000 for Buchan, whereby Arsenal would pay £2,000 initially, plus £100 for each goal he scored in his debut season. Sunderland agreed, the terms of the transfer attracting huge publicity. Since Buchan finished the campaign with 20 goals in League and FA Cup, the club ended up paying Sunderland £4,000 anyway – although it was widely but erroneously reported, and continues to be reiterated, that Buchan scored 21 and Arsenal paid £100 more than they needed to. That certainly made for good newspaper copy – and either way, the value of the publicity was priceless in raising Arsenal's profile, which is no doubt what Norris and Chapman had intended.

3 Tom Whittaker, who was 29 at the time – younger than some of the players – but whose interest in physiotherapy and progressive approach to healing injuries had impressed Chapman and signalled a radical departure from the prevailing 'bucket and sponge' culture. Effectively demoted for his presumption, Hardy – who'd been hired by Sir Henry Norris – promptly left Arsenal and joined Tottenham Hotspur as trainer.

4 Cliff Bastin, who was initially reluctant, but convinced by Chapman's powers of persuasion and was soon creating history from his new position.

5 Aston Villa.

6 David Jack – who netted a staggering 14 goals in that 9-match spree.

7 Arsenal's victims at Highbury on 9 January 1932 were Darwen. The goal-scorers were Cliff Bastin (4), David Jack (3), Joe Hulme (2) and Jack Lambert (2).

8 Tommy Black, Charlie Walsh and Billy Warnes. Black, who had particularly angered Chapman by rashly conceding a penalty, was sold to Plymouth Argyle less than a week later, while Warnes was transferred to Norwich within three weeks and Walsh left for Brentford at the end of the season.

9 Ted Drake (Southampton); Wilf Copping (Leeds United); Jack Crayston (Bradford Park Avenue).

10 Alf Kirchen, who scored 45 goals in 101 appearances for Arsenal and 2 in 3 for England before the Second World War intervened, and a further 80 in 113 games for the club during the war, when he served as a PT instructor with the RAF. After suffering a serious knee injury in a wartime match that ended his football career, Alf returned to farming, represented England at clay pigeon shooting and became Honorary President of the Norfolk Arsenal Supporters Club.

11 Eddie Carr, a miner from County Durham, who made only one more first-team appearance for the club before injury, then the Second World War, sabotaged his Arsenal career. He joined Huddersfield Town in 1945.

Four Four Two

Four

1 Paul Davis (1993–95), Patrick Vieira (1996–2005), Cesc Fabregas (2006–11) and Per Mertesacker (since 2011).

2 Theo Walcott, Alexis Sanchez, Per Mertesacker and Olivier Giroud were on target against Villa in the triumphant 2015 FA Cup final.

3 Arsenal have finished fourth six times during Arsene Wenger's reign: in 2005/06 (with 67 points), 2006/07 (68 points), 2008/09 (72 points), 2010/11 (68 pts), 2012/13 (73 points) and 2013/14 (79 points).

4 Ted Drake, who scored exactly 4 goals in a match on six occasions, and whose 139-goal total as a Gunner also included one 7-goal haul.

Four

5 Yaya Sanogo.

6 Omonia Nicosia (h), Everton (a), Manchester City (a) and Sampdoria (a).

7 Ju Young Park started the match, while Ryo Miyaichi, Oguzhan Ozyakup and Chuks Aneke came on as substitutes.

8 (1) Wolves; (2) Coventry City; (3) West Bromwich Albion; (4) Nottingham Forest.

Two
9 Frankie Simek and Danny Karbassiyoon.

10 Newcastle United (1932, 1952 and 1998) and Liverpool (1950, 1971 and 2001).

... and a goalie
11 Wojciech Szczesny and Petr Cech. The pair were joint winners in 2013/14 – when Cech was at Chelsea – with sixteen clean sheets apiece. Subsequently Cech won it in 2015/16 – his first season as a Gunner – again with sixteen. He'd also won in 2004/05 with twenty-one clean sheets for Chelsea, and was a winner again with the Blues in 2009/10 (seventeen).

1 Up to the end of November 2016, forty-nine players had scored 50 or more goals for Arsenal, Alexis Sanchez becoming the latest to join this elite group when he scored his second at Sunderland on 29 October 2016. Best-placed among the 2016/17 squad to break the 50-goal barrier is Aaron Ramsey on 43.

2 (1) David Jack scored 26 goals in thirty-six games in 1928/29; (2) Joe Baker 31 in forty-two, 1962/63; (3) Malcolm Macdonald 29 in fifty, 1976/77; Ian Wright 26 in thirty-three, 1991/92; Alexis Sanchez 25 in fifty-two, 2014/15.

3 Ray Kennedy (Fairs Cup 1st leg v Anderlecht, 1970); Eddie Kelly, John Radford and Jon Sammels (Fairs Cup, 2nd leg v Anderlecht, 1970); Alan Smith (Cup Winners' Cup v Parma, 1994); John Hartson (Cup Winners' Cup v Real Zaragoza, 1995); Sol Campbell (Champions League v Barcelona, 2006).

4 Bob Turnbull, who scored 14 goals in his first ten games
after switching to centre-forward. Sadly, he only managed 7
goals the next season, and none at all the season after that.

5 Leicester City in a 5–2 away win on 26 September 2015.
Sanchez became the first player to score hat-tricks in each
of the Premier League, La Liga and Serie A.

6 Theo Walcott.

7 58 – Henry scored 39 and Pires 19.

8 Henry White (1921/22), Jimmy Brain (1927/28), Ted Drake
(1934/35) and Reg Lewis (1946/47).

9 Jimmy Brain, Jack Lambert and Ted Drake each scored
twelve hat-tricks for Arsenal, with Drake's haul including
one double hat-trick.

10 Henry Edward 'Harry' King.

11 (1) Robin van Persie with 37; (2) Theo Walcott, 21; (3)
Olivier Giroud, 22; (4) Alexis Sanchez, 25; (5) Giroud, 24.

Last Line of Defence

1   (1) Fred Beardsley v Lyndhurst (won 11–0, home) FA Cup
    Qualifying Competition, 1st Round, 5 October 1889; (2)
    Charlie Williams v Newcastle United (2–2, home) Division
    2, 2 September 1893; (3) Jim Furnell v Gillingham (1–1,
    home) League Cup 2nd Round, 13 September 1966; (4) Ian
    McKechnie v Staevnet (7–1, away) Inter-Cities Fairs Cup 1st
    Round, 1st leg, 25 September 1963.
2   Jimmy Rimmer.
3   Harry Storer, for the Football League in 1895.
4   In chronological order: David Seaman, John Lukic, Lee
    Harper, Alex Manninger, Stuart Taylor, Richard Wright, Rami
    Shaaban, Jens Lehmann, Graham Stack, Manuel Almunia,
    Mart Poom, Lukasz Fabianski, Vito Mannone, Wojciech
    Szczesny, Emiliano Martinez, David Ospina, Petr Cech.
5   Scotsman Hugh Laughlan McDonald, who joined Woolwich
    Arsenal in 1906 from Beith, was transferred to Brighton
    and rejoined Arsenal in 1908. He joined Oldham (1910)
    but returned to Arsenal from Bradford (1912) and made
    the last of his 103 appearances as a Gunner against Spurs in
    April 1913 before joining Fulham in November 1913.
6   Geoff Barnett, who was between the posts for the Everton
    youth team that beat Arsenal 3–2 on aggregate in 1964/65,
    joined Arsenal in 1969 and stood in for the injured Bob
    Wilson during the 1972 FA Cup final against Leeds United.

7 Leigh Roose – aka 'Dr' Leigh Richmond 'Dick' Roose, MM – who also played for Stoke, Everton, Sunderland and Aston Villa, among other clubs. He remained an amateur throughout his career, enabling him to run up a creative expense account, and exploited the freedom of goalkeepers to handle the ball anywhere in their own half so effectively that the FA introduced a significant rule change in 1912 to curb him. Consequently goalkeepers can only handle the ball within their penalty area.

8 Jack Kelsey, who made a then record 352 appearances for Arsenal, won a League championship medal in 1952/53, was injured playing for Wales against Brazil, and became Arsenal's commercial manager.

9 Bill Harper.

10 Jens Lehmann, who made those penalty saves in the Community Shield, Champions League semi-final and FA Cup final, respectively.

11 David Seaman (who made 17 appearances), Richard Wright (12) and Stuart Taylor (9 plus 1 as substitute for Wright in the final match v Everton, which enabled him to qualify for a medal).

Tom Whittaker at the Helm (1947–56)

1 Planning and preparing vehicles for the D-Day landings on Normandy beaches.

2 Archie Macaulay from Brentford and Don Roper from Southampton.

3 Right-back George Male, who made 318 appearances and following retirement coached Arsenal's young players, was chief scout and filled various other administrative roles for the club.

4 Division 2 club Bradford Park Avenue, who won 1–0 at Highbury.

5 Joe Mercer, whose manager at Everton, Theo Kelly, refused to accept he was injured and was happy to sell him, telling the press Mercer's career was over and he wouldn't last six months at Arsenal. Helped by Whittaker's healing skills, Mercer made 275 appearances and led the Gunners to three major trophies.

6 Ronnie Rooke, then aged 36.

7 They won the cup without having to leave London, receiving home draws in each round, meeting Chelsea at White Hart Lane in the semi-final and replay, and beating Liverpool at Wembley.

8 Freddie Cox, who scored in each of the 4 matches, including a brace in the 1952 replay which Arsenal won 3–0.

9 Jimmy Logie

10 (1) Jimmy Logie; (2) Ray Daniel; (3) Walley Barnes – who didn't play again for eighteen months.

11 Pete Goring (10 goals in 29 appearances), Jimmy Logie (10 in 32), Don Roper (14 in 41), Cliff Holton (19 in 21), Doug Lishman (22 in 39).

Spot the
Connection #1

1 Peter Marinello.
2 Igors Stepanovs.
3 Derek Tapscott.
4 Alberto Mendez.
5 George Eastham.
6 Thomas Vermaelen.
7 Ronnie Rooke.
8 Freddie Ljungberg.
9 Ian Wright.
10 Gilberto Silva.
11 They all scored on their competitive first-team debuts for
   Arsenal. (1) Marinello v Manchester United, 7 January 1970;
   (2) Stepanovs v Ipswich, 1 November 2000; (3) Tapscott v
   Liverpool, 10 April 1954; (4) Mendez v Birmingham City,
   14 October 1997; (5) Eastham v Bolton, 10 December
   1960; (6) Vermaelen v Everton, 15 August 2009; (7)
   Rooke v Charlton, 14 December 1946; (8) Ljungberg v
   Manchester United, 20 September 1998; (9) Wright v
   Leicester, 25 September 1991; (10) Gilberto v Liverpool,
   11 August 2002.

The Wenger Decades (1996–2016)

1 Remi Garde, who joined Arsenal from Strasbourg on 14 August 1996, the same day that Patrick Vieira signed from AC Milan. They had been signed on Wenger's recommendation while Le Professor was seeing out his contract with Nagoya Grampus Eight in Japan.

2 Seaman; Dixon, Keown, Bould, Adams, Winterburn; Platt, Vieira, Merson; Wright, Hartson (Parlour). Unused substitutes: Shaw, Linighan, Rose, Lukic.

3 Ian Wright (penalty), Tony Adams and Dennis Bergkamp.

4 Six; no other Arsenal manager won the cup more than once.

5 He became the first foreign manager to win the championship.

6 They scored in every one of their 38 Premier League matches; previously the club record had been 31 consecutive matches in 1931. Arsenal then extended the record for scoring in consecutive matches to 55.

7 The Chelsea dozen are (1) Ruud Gullit (May 1996–February 1998), who was the Blues' boss at the time of Arsene Wenger's appointment; (2) Gianluca Vialli (Feb 1998–Sept 2000); (3) Claudio Ranieri (Sept 2000–May 2004); (4) José Mourinho (June 2004–Sept 2007 and June 2013–Dec 2015); (5) Avram Grant (Sept 2007–May 2008); (6) Luiz Felipe Scolari (July 2008–Feb 2009); (7) Guus Hiddink (Feb 2009–May 2009 and Dec 2015–May 2016); (8) Carlo Ancelotti (July 2009–May 2011); (9) Andre Villas–Boas (June 2011–March 2012); (10) Roberto Di Matteo (March 2012–Nov 2012); (11) Rafael Benitez (Nov 2012–May 2013); and (12) Antonio Conte since July 2016.

8 Arsenal's stellar performance at Fratton Park against Redknapp's Portsmouth in an FA Cup 6th Round tie on 6 March 2004. The Gunners won 5–1, and the Pompey fans gave them a standing ovation.

9 Everton visited Highbury on 11 May 2005 as Arsenal completed their home League programme. The following season was to be the last at the famous old stadium, and Arsenal would wear 'redcurrant' shirts throughout in a nod to their 1913 kit. The Gunners swept Everton aside 7–0. A contract extension had yet to be agreed with Dennis Bergkamp, who underlined his enduring value by scoring an outstanding goal and setting up 3 more. Between the posts for the Toffees was former Arsenal keeper Richard Wright, while future Gunners' captain Mikel Arteta was in midfield.

10 Thierry Henry scoring the winning goal at the Emirates in an FA Cup 3rd Round tie against Leeds United on 9 January 2012 – on his return to the club on loan from New York Red Bulls. Henry had come on as a 68th-minute substitute and 10 minutes later scored his 227th Arsenal goal, five years after his 226th, as the Gunners won 1–0.

11 The FA Cup when Arsenal won it in 2014 to end a nine-year wait for silverware.

Seventeen
Years of Hurt

1 Twelfth in 1953/54, having come first the previous season.
2 Tommy Lawton, who was signed from Brentford and scored 15 goals in 38 appearances.
3 Alec Stock – who had enjoyed FA Cup giant-killing success with Yeovil Town and would experience further highs at QPR and Fulham.
4 Arsenal were beaten 3–1 and eliminated from the FA Cup at the first hurdle by Northampton Town, a team from Division 3 South. The 3rd Round exit came in the midst of a run of one win in eight games.
5 Arsenal finished third in 1958/59, George Swindin's first season as manager, and goalkeeper Jack Kelsey suffered a broken arm against Sheffield United in the cup.
6 Having been drawn away to Second Division Rotherham United in the 3rd Round, Arsenal drew 2–2 at Millmoor and 1–1 in the Highbury replay before losing a second replay 2–0 on Sheffield Wednesday's ground.
7 George Eastham, whose transfer from Newcastle United saw Bloomfield sign for Birmingham City in November 1960.
8 Arsenal's potent attack (typically MacLeod, Strong, Baker, Eastham, Armstrong) racked up 90 goals – the second-highest post-war total, exceeded only in the 1952/53 title-winning campaign – but was let down by a porous defence that shipped 82 goals, leaving Billy Wright's team out of contention in eighth place.

9 Northern Ireland international Derek Dougan, who scored one of Peterborough's goals against the Gunners.

10 Arsenal adopted a new kit design that dispensed with the trademark white sleeves and made them fairly indistinguishable from the likes of Nottingham Forest, Bristol City or Barnsley. It was presented to fans as something the players had requested; fortunately the players wanted to revert to red with white sleeves by the time the 1967/68 season kicked off.

11 Joe Baker scored his 100th and last Arsenal goal in a 5–2 victory over Sheffield Wednesday at Highbury on 28 December 1965.

London Pride

1 Eleven – Brentford, Charlton Athletic, Chelsea, Crystal
   Palace, Fulham, Leyton Orient (including as Clapton
   Orient), Millwall, Queen's Park Rangers, Tottenham
   Hotspur, West Ham United and Wimbledon.

2 Chelsea – at Stamford Bridge on 9 November 1907, and
   Arsenal lost 1–2. Until then the club's only other southern
   opponents in League fixtures had been Luton Town (from
   1897) and Bristol City (from 1901).

3 Chelsea (2–1) on 28 November 1908 at Stamford Bridge.

4 In sequence, the results and scorers were 5–1 (h) v QPR
   (Rix 2, Brady, Stapleton 2); 5–0 (a) v Spurs (Sunderland
   3, Stapleton, Brady); 2–1 (a) v QPR (Price, Brady); 1–0
   (h) v Spurs (Stapleton); 5–2 (h) v Chelsea (Stapleton 2,
   O'Leary, Sunderland, Price); 1–1 (a) v Chelsea (Macdonald).
   At the end of that season, Chelsea (twenty-second) and
   QPR (twentieth) were relegated. Spurs finished eleventh;
   Arsenal were seventh and FA Cup winners.

5 (1) Leslie Knighton – Arsenal manager 1919–25, Chelsea
   boss 1933–39; (2) Ted Drake – Arsenal player 1934–45,
   Chelsea manager 1952–61; (3) Tommy Docherty – Arsenal
   player 1958–61, Chelsea manager 1961–67; (4) Dave
   Sexton – Arsenal coach 1966–67, Chelsea manager 1967–
   74; (5) John Hollins – Arsenal player 1979–83, Chelsea
   manager 1985–88; (6) Bobby Campbell – Arsenal coach
   1973–76, Chelsea manager 1988–91.

6 (1) Arsenal 6–0 Charlton, 3 September 1947; (2) Chelsea 1–5 Arsenal, 29 November 1930; (3) Arsenal 7–0 Crystal Palace, 27 January 1934; (4) QPR 0–6 Arsenal, 27 January 2001; (5) Tottenham 0–6 Arsenal, 6 March 1935; (6) Arsenal 6–1 West Ham, 20 March 1976.

7 (1) Ted Drake; (2) Ben Marden; (3) John Radford; (4) Kanu; (5) Robin van Persie.

8 John Radford between 1969 and 1973.

9 (1) Jim Standen; (2) Pat Jennings and Jimmy Robertson; (3) John Hollins and Tommy Baldwin; (4) Bobby Gould (manager) and Don Howe (coach); (5) Sol Campbell and George Graham (manager); (6) Petr Cech and Cesc Fabregas.

10 Sylvain Wiltord.

11 (1) QPR – against whom Arsenal's home League record as at 30 November 2016 was P23 W15 D6 L2; (2) Crystal Palace: P16 W12 D3 L1; (3) Fulham: P27 W22 D5 L0.

Back with a Bang – Mee and McLintock Restore the Glory

1 Bertie Mee asked the chairman for the option to revert to his previous position after twelve months if things were not working out; this was agreed, and reflected in his official title as acting manager during the first year of his tenure.

2 Dave Sexton joined from Fulham as first-team coach, and in the transfer market Mee signed Colin Addison, George Graham and Bob McNab from Nottingham Forest, Chelsea and Huddersfield Town, respectively.

3 Ian Ure (to Manchester United, August 1969); Jimmy Robertson (Ipswich, March 1970); Bobby Gould (Wolves, June 1970), Terry Neill (Hull City as player-manager, June 1970); and David Court (Luton, July 1970).

4 Charlie George, Eddie Kelly and Ray Kennedy.

5 Charlie George.

6 Four goals, achieved on four occasions, all at Highbury: 4–0 v Manchester United, Nottingham Forest and Everton; and 6–2 v West Bromwich Albion.

7 Peter Simpson, who was an integral part – and arguably the most underrated member of – the first Double-winning team. He made 478 appearances and scored 15 goals for Arsenal between his debut in 1964 as a 19 year old and his final match in January 1978.

"IT WAS MY AIM TO PLAY WITH A SMILE, FOR FUN, AS AN ENTERTAINMENT. IF YOU CAN MAKE THE SUPPORTERS HAPPY YOU ARE DOING THE JOB CORRECTLY."

CHARLIE GEORGE
1950–1975

FOREVER REMEMBERED FOR HIS WINNING GOAL IN THE 1971 FA CUP FINAL, CHARLIE PLAYED 179 TIMES FOR THE CLUB, SCORING 49 GOALS. AN ISLINGTON BOY, HE WAS A PERENNIAL FANS' FAVOURITE.

THE FANS

EIGHTEEN STORIES OF THE LUCKY AND OFF TO THE GAME.

CLOCK END

8 Arsenal were drawn away in every round – although they did have three replays at Highbury and 7 matches on neutral grounds, including semi-finals and finals.

9 Peter Storey.

10 Arsenal beat eventual champions Liverpool 2–0 at Anfield on 10 February 1973 with Alan Ball (penalty) and John Radford the scorers. But eventual winners Sunderland beat the Gunners 2–1 in the cup.

11 403 (scoring 32 goals).

Four Three Three

Four

1 Emmanuel Petit, Patrick Vieira, Thierry Henry (a Monaco player at the time, joining Arsenal from Juventus in August 1999), and Robert Pires (with Metz in 1998, soon to join Marseille from whom he signed for Arsenal in 2000).

2 Cliff Holton, who made his League debut on Boxing Day 1950 and was transferred to Watford in October 1958 having made 217 appearances. He became Watford's highest League scorer in a season (42 in 1959/60), and repeated the feat at Northampton Town (36 in 1961/62); both records still stand.

3 The most recent was Andrey Arshavin, who scored all 4 in a 4–4 draw at Liverpool on 21 April 2009. He was the first since Thierry Henry hit 4 in a 5–0 home win over Leeds United on 16 April 2004. Before that Ian Wright scored all 4 in a 4–2 home win over Everton on 21 December 1991; and Tony Woodcock netted 5 in a 6–2 Arsenal win at Aston Villa on 29 October 1983.

4 Lazio (Italy), Sturm Graz (Austria), Beveren Waas (Belgium) and Cologne (West Germany).

Three

5 David Herd (107 goals in 180 Arsenal appearances between 1954 and 1961); Frank Stapleton (108 in 300, 1975–81); and Robin van Persie (132 in 278, 2004–12).

6 Santi Cazorla, Laurent Koscielny and Aaron Ramsey.
7 Southampton – Jos Hooiveld and Nathaniel Clyne when Arsenal beat Saints 6–1 at Emirates Stadium on 15 September 2012; Guilherme Do Prado in the 1–1 draw at St Mary's on New Year's Day 2013.

Three
8 John Hartson, Rhys Weston and Aaron Ramsey.
9 The three ex-Gunners among Leeds United's 1991/92 title-winning squad were John Lukic (who made 42 appearances), Chris Whyte (41) and Lee Chapman (38).
10 Schalke 04, Werder Bremen and Real Madrid.

... and a goalie
11 The leading appearance-makers among Arsenal goalkeepers are (1) David Seaman with 564; (2) Jack Kelsey, 352; (3) Pat Jennings, 327. Those who've kept the most clean sheets are (1) Seaman with 237; (2) Bob Wilson (125 from 308 appearances); and (3) John Lukic, who had 114 shut-outs in 298 appearances.

Make Mine a Double

1 (a) Leeds United; Manchester United; Liverpool; (b) Liverpool; Newcastle United; Chelsea.
2 It was the first time a club had won the FA Cup before clinching the League title.
3 64 (42 League, 9 FA Cup, 5 League Cup and 8 Fairs Cup).
4 1970/71: Ray Kennedy (21), John Radford (17), George Graham (12) and Charlie George (10); 1997/98: Dennis Bergkamp (19), Marc Overmars (14) and Ian Wright (10); 2001/02: Thierry Henry (25), Freddie Ljungberg (14), Dennis Bergkamp (12), Sylvain Wiltord (12) and Robert Pires (10).

5 Blackburn Rovers, who won 3–1 at Highbury (but were thrashed 4–1 at Ewood Park over Easter as Arsenal closed in on the title).

6 Bergkamp's 3 goals were subsequently voted first, second and third by viewers in BBC TV *Match of the Day*'s 'Goal of the Month' competition.

7 5–0 – a scoreline they achieved twice: at home to Barnsley on 4 October 1997 and at home to Wimbledon on 18 April 1998.

8 Three – against Port Vale (away) in the 3rd Round, Crystal Palace (away) in the 5th, and West Ham United (away) in the 6th.

9 Frank McLintock (1970/71); Dennis Bergkamp (1997/98); Robert Pires (2001/02).

10 Patrick Vieira (35 starts +1 appearance as substitute); Thierry Henry (31+2); Sol Campbell (29+2); Ashley Cole (29); Robert Pires (27+1); Lauren (27); Ray Parlour (25+2); Freddie Ljungberg (24+1); Sylvain Wiltord (23+10); Dennis Bergkamp (22+11); Martin Keown (21+1); David Seaman (17); Oleg Luzhny (15+3); Gio van Bronckhorst (13+8); Richard Wright (12); Gilles Grimandi (11+15); Matthew Upson (10+4); Tony Adams (10); Kanu (9+14); Stuart Taylor (9+1); Edu (8+6); Lee Dixon (3+10). Three other players made League appearances, but not enough to qualify for a medal: Igors Stepanovs (6), Francis Jeffers (2+4) and Jeremie Aliadiere (0+1).

11 Arsenal are the only club to win the Double both before and after the advent of the Premier League; and they are also the only club to have done the Double in more than one decade.

Round 19

Terry Neill's Red and White (and Green) Army

1 On 6 October 1973, in a League match against Birmingham City at Highbury, Brady was introduced as a substitute for Jeff Blockley.

2 307 appearances, 59 goals.

3 The 1978 FA Cup final when Brady, carrying an ankle injury, was not fully fit and had to be replaced by substitute Graham Rix. Arsenal lost 1–0 to Ipswich Town, and Brady's disappointment was laced with guilt that he hadn't ruled himself out of contention prior to the match.

4 Arsenal played eleven FA Cup matches in 1979 and eleven more in 1980. Their opponents in 1979 were Sheffield Wednesday, Notts County, Nottingham Forest, Southampton, Wolverhampton Wanderers and Manchester United. In 1980 they met Cardiff City, Brighton & Hove Albion, Bolton Wanderers, Watford, Liverpool and West Ham United.

5 Pat Jennings, Pat Rice, Sammy Nelson, David O'Leary, Liam Brady and Frank Stapleton played in all four (Nelson once as a substitute), while John Devine appeared once.

6 Pat Jennings, Willie Young and substitute Steve Walford.

7 Alan Sunderland and Brian Talbot, with Talbot being credited with the goal.

8 Arsenal drew 1–1 with Chelsea at Stamford Bridge.

9 Willie Young, whose foul probably prevented West Ham from scoring a second goal, and who therefore earned the gratitude of Gooners by putting the team first. The sanctimonious media's apoplexy was fuelled by the fact that Allen, at 17 already the youngest FA Cup finalist, would have added to the perceived romance of the occasion by scoring at Wembley. FIFA's outlawing of the professional foul nine years later is widely attributed to Young's intervention in 1980.

10 (1) The Heysel Stadium, Brussels; (2) Alfredo di Stefano; (3) it was the first time any European final had been decided by penalties, and the only time the Cup Winners' Cup final was.

11 Arsenal had to play no fewer than 17 matches – including six semi-finals and two finals – which worked out as a game every 2.8 days for six and a half weeks, with no let-up and a small squad by today's standards. In both cup finals and their last League game, in which victory would have secured a UEFA Cup place the following season, the players simply looked jaded; there just wasn't enough fuel left in the tank.

Trivia Pursuit #2

First and Last

1 Ian Selley and Nicolas Anelka. In the 85th minute, Selley came on for Patrick Vieira and Anelka for Ian Wright. Selley was making his first Arsenal appearance since breaking a leg against Leicester in February 1995; it proved to be his final outing as a Gunner before being sold to Fulham. Anelka's introduction from the bench marked his Arsenal debut.

2 Tommy Docherty, who was signed by new manager George Swindin from Preston on 23 August 1958, scored against Burnley in a 3–0 Highbury win three days later, never scored again in 90 appearances, then joined Chelsea as player-coach under Ted Drake in February 1961, taking over from Ted as manager later that year. It was the first of fifteen managerial appointments 'The Doc' took up before retiring in 1988.

Scot-Free

3 Defender Scott Marshall. The Edinburgh-born son of former Hearts and Newcastle goalkeeper Gordon came on as substitute for Gilles Grimandi in the 51st minute of Arsenal's 0–2 away defeat by Sheffield Wednesday on 22 November 1997. It was his twenty-sixth and final first-team appearance (including six as a substitute) before his transfer to Southampton in August 1998.

X Factor
4 Graham Rix, Lee Dixon and Alex Oxlade-Chamberlain.

Book Club
5 (1) Dennis Bergkamp; (2) Jack Kelsey; (3) Tony Adams;
   (4) Eddie Hapgood; (5) Frank McLintock; (6) Peter Storey;
   (7) Paul Merson; (8) Bernard Joy; (9) George Graham;
   (10) Mel Charles; (11) Jon Sammels.

Family Affair
6 (1) Bobby and George; (2) Les and Denis; (3) Danny and
   Denis; (4) Justin and Gavin; (5) Michael and Tommy.

S Club 7

7 (1) Sunderland; (2) Southampton; (3) Swansea City;
(4) Stoke City; (5) Sheffield Wednesday; (6) Sampdoria;
(7) Sevilla.

Utility Man

8 Alf Baker, an ex-miner, who was signed by Leslie Knighton
for Arsenal in 1919 and became a key member of Herbert
Chapman's early teams, earning an FA Cup runners-up
medal in 1927 and a winner's medal three years later in his
penultimate appearance for the club, for whom he later
worked as a scout.

3–2–1

9 (1) Junichi Inamoto, Carlin Itonga and Alex Iwobi;
(U) Matthew Upson and Ian Ure; (Z) Gedion Zelalem.

Double-barrelled

10 Jay Emmanuel-Thomas; Ainsley Maitland-Niles; Quincy
Owusu-Abeyie; Alex Oxlade-Chamberlain; Jeff Reine-
Adelaide.

a.k.a.

11 (1) Archie Gray; (2) Peter Storey; (3) Les Compton; (4) Alf
Baker; (5) Billy McCullough; (6) David Rocastle; (7) Frank
Hill; (8) Peter Simpson; (9) George Graham; (10) George
Armstrong; (11) Thierry Henry.

1 George Graham's 1990/91 title winners lost just 1 match, while George Allison's 1937/38 side suffered eleven defeats but still finished as champions.
2 Arsenal would have earned 94 points in both 1930–31 (28 wins, 10 draws) and 1970/71 (29 wins, 7 draws) – although they were both 42-match campaigns compared with 38 in 2003/04.
3 Jack Lambert scored 38 and David Jack scored 31, while Cliff Bastin (who scored 28) was ever-present.
4 Six straight wins – and they were unbeaten over the first 17 matches of the campaign.

5 Bolton Wanderers in both 1931 and 1938; Grimsby Town in 1948; and Coventry City in 1991.

6 Blackpool (1–0 home, 1–0 away), Burnley (1–0, 2–1), Coventry City (1–0, 3–1), Ipswich Town (3–2, 1–0), Manchester City (1–0, 2–0), Manchester United (4–0, 3–1), Nottingham Forest (4–0, 3–0), Tottenham Hotspur (2–0, 1–0), and Wolverhampton Wanderers (2–1, 3–0).

7 Lee Dixon, Nigel Winterburn, Steve Bould, Tony Adams, David O'Leary, Michael Thomas, Paul Davis, David Rocastle, Alan Smith, Paul Merson and Perry Groves.

8 In winning the League in 1990/91, Arsenal conceded only 18 goals. In contrast, when they won the title in 1952/53, their defence was breached sixty-four times – but they still secured the championship on goal average.

9 (1) Charlie George scored the first and Ray Kennedy the last; (2) Brian Marwood and Michael Thomas; (3) Paul Merson and Perry Groves; (4) Ian Wright and Tony Adams; (5) Thierry Henry and Francis Jeffers; (6) Thierry Henry (penalty) and Patrick Vieira.

10 53 – Hulme scored 20 and Bastin 33. (Ernie Coleman was second top scorer with 24 goals.)

11 Alan Smith, who headed Arsenal's first goal at Anfield to finish the season as the First Division's top scorer with 23, having begun the campaign by netting in each of the Gunners' first 8 matches.

It's Happened Again ...

1 Woolwich Arsenal beat Spurs 1–0 in a Division 1 match at the Manor Ground on 4 December 1909, Walter Lawrence claiming the distinction of scoring the first ever derby goal.

2 The first time Arsenal and Spurs met as north London neighbours separated by a mere 4 miles was on 15 January 1921, when Spurs beat Arsenal 2–1 in a First Division fixture that came close to being postponed because of thick fog inside White Hart Lane.

3 Jimmy Brain headed the only goal of the game as Arsenal beat Spurs 1–0 at Highbury on 25 October 1924, his first appearance in the first-team. He netted 139 goals for the Gunners overall, placing him joint fifth on the all-time list, and earned a medal with 16 appearances in Arsenal's first title-winning season of 1930/31. He left to join Spurs in September 1931 but only played forty-seven times for them, scoring 10 goals, before leaving in 1934.

4 Alan Sunderland, Robert Pires and Emmanuel Adebayor each scored 8 goals against Spurs, followed by David Herd and John Radford on 7, and Joe Baker and Ian Wright on 6.

5 It was a charity cricket match between Arsenal and Spurs players in aid of the Woodberry Down Boys Club. The teams competed for the Austin Morris Empire Trophy. Arsenal amassed 178 runs from 30 overs, Geoff Barnett top-scoring with 67, then bowled their opponents out for 160 with Bob McNab taking two Spurs wickets for 19 runs. Managers Bertie Mee and Bill Nicholson umpired the match.

6 Mathieu Flamini.

7 In the two League meetings against Tottenham, Olivier Giroud scored the winner in the 1–0 home win, Tomas Rosicky scored the decisive goal in the 1–0 away win, and in the FA Cup 3rd Round tie between the teams, Rosicky and Santi Cazorla were on target in a 2–0 win.

8 Robert Pires, in each of Arsenal's away games at the Lane from 2001/02 until and including 2005/06.

9 It was fellow Frenchman Jacques Santini, who took charge of just thirteen Spurs games before controversially quitting in November 2004.

10 Thierry Henry, Lauren (a penalty), Patrick Vieira, Freddie Ljungberg and Robert Pires.

11 Arsenal have beaten Spurs eleven times in cup matches, drawing 3 and losing 5. Seven of the wins have come in 13 League Cup matches, and four have been in six FA Cup meetings.

1 Martin Keown, who was transferred to Aston Villa in July 1986 for £200,000 after Graham rejected his request for a wage increase, but bought back from Everton for £2 million in 1993, going on to win many major honours.

2 Perry Groves from Colchester United for a reported fee of £50,000 in September 1986.

3 (1) Arsenal beat Liverpool 2–1; (2) Charlie Nicholas scored both Arsenal goals after Ian Rush had put Liverpool ahead; (3) Kenny Sansom was captain; (4) Perry Groves replaced Niall Quinn and Michael Thomas replaced Martin Hayes; (5) Thomas had made his debut as a substitute against Spurs in the first leg of the semi-final, replacing Gus Caesar.

4 Wimbledon – the Gunners beat the FA Cup holders 5–1 at Plough Lane on 27 August 1988, then beat the Dons 3–0 on the same ground on 25 August 1990.

5 The five players who scored 1 crucial goal apiece during the 1988/89 League title success were (1) Kevin Richardson in a 3–1 win at Everton; (2) Paul Davis in a 2–2 draw at home to Charlton; (3 & 4) Lee Dixon and Niall Quinn, who scored the goals in a 2–0 home win against Everton; and (5) Martin Hayes who netted the only goal of the game at Middlesbrough.

6 No fewer than six: home (1–1) and away (2–0) in League Division 1; the semi-final of the Mercantile Credit Centenary Trophy (2–1); and three times in the 3rd Round of the League Cup – at Anfield (1–1), Highbury (0–0) and Villa Park (1–2).

7 Goalkeeper David Seaman from QPR, centre-back Andy Linighan from Norwich and Swedish winger Anders Limpar from Cremonese.

8 Firstly they were deducted 2 points by the Football League for their part in a brawl on the Old Trafford pitch; secondly captain Tony Adams was given a prison sentence for drink-driving and was consequently unavailable for eight crucial League games.

9 The 3–1 defeat by Benfica in the second leg of Arsenal's 2nd Round European Cup tie. The defeat is credited by many, including several members of the team, with ushering in a more cautious and attritional phase involving less midfield creativity, which served Arsenal well in cup football but limited their impact in the League.

10 (1) John Jensen was the only player to start both the Premier League game against Wednesday on 6 May 1993 and the FA Cup Final against them on 15 May; (2) the line-ups for the two matches were: League – Miller, Lydersen (Flatts), Keown, Marshall, O'Leary, Bould, Jensen (McGowan), Selley, Smith, Heaney, Carter. FA Cup – Seaman, Dixon, Winterburn, Davis, Linighan, Adams, Jensen, Wright (O'Leary), Campbell, Merson, Parlour (Smith).

11 Paul Davis.

Spot the
Connection #2

1 Peter Kyle.
2 Bob John.
3 David Jack.
4 Alex James.
5 Ray Daniel.
6 Mel Charles.
7 George Graham.
8 Charlie George.
9 Charlie Nicholas.
10 Michael Thomas.
11 This was a bit of a crafty, 'hiding in plain sight' link, as the connection shared by all ten of the Arsenal stars is simply that their surnames are also common first names. Sorry!

Invincible! The 2003/04 Season

1 Jens Lehmann (38 appearances), Lauren (32), Ashley Cole (32), Sol Campbell (35), Kolo Toure (37), Patrick Vieira (29), Gilberto Silva (32), Freddie Ljungberg (30), Robert Pires (36), Dennis Bergkamp (28), Thierry Henry (37), Edu (30), Ray Parlour (25), Pascal Cygan (18), José Antonio Reyes (13), Sylvain Wiltord (12), Gael Clichy (12), Kanu (10), Jeremie Aliadiere (10), Martin Keown (10).

2 The goalless draw at Old Trafford in which Manchester United failed to convert a late penalty and several players were subsequently punished for their conduct at the final whistle.

3 Inter Milan were beaten 5–1 at the San Siro, Arsenal's goals being scored by Henry (2), Ljungberg, Edu and Pires.

4 They all played for Arsenal in two different spells – Campbell 2001–06 and 2010; Henry 1999–2007 and 2012; Keown 1981–86 and 1993–2004; Lehmann 2003–08 and 2011.

5 Oleg Luzhny.

6 Sami Hyypia sliced Edu's header into his own net before Robert Pires curled in a stupendous shot from some 30 yards at Anfield in October; and Pires was on target again at Highbury in May, scoring resilient Arsenal's second in a pivotal game that saw Thierry Henry claim a hat-trick featuring one of the goals of the season.

7 Martin Keown, who often said a few words to the team before matches, but this time asked and was given the go-ahead by Arsene Wenger to address the players at half-time in an effort to help lift them with a season's excellent work threatening to unravel.

8 Leeds 1–4 Arsenal on 1 November 2003 (Henry 2, Pires, Gilberto); Leeds 1–4 Arsenal on 4 January 2004 in the FA Cup 3rd Round (Henry, Edu, Pires, Toure); Arsenal 5–0 Leeds on 16 April 2004 (Pires, Henry 4 – 1 penalty). Jermaine Pennant, on loan from the Gunners, faced them both times in the League.

9 August – Kolo Toure; September – Kolo Toure; October – Thierry Henry; November – Thierry Henry; December – Robert Pires; January – Thierry Henry; February – Edu; March – Thierry Henry; April – Thierry Henry; May – Patrick Vieira.

10 Four: v Birmingham (home), 0–0; v Portsmouth (away), 1–1; v Fulham (away) 1–0; v Leicester City (home), 2–1.

11 (1) Middlesbrough (won 5–3); (2) Blackburn Rovers (won 3–0); (3) Aston Villa (won 3–1).

The 'WM' Formation

1 Richard Wright, who joined Arsenal from Ipswich and made all his appearances during the 2001/02 Double-winning campaign before moving to Everton.

2 Northern Ireland internationals Jimmy Magill, who made 131 Arsenal appearances during his 1959–65 stint at the club, and Billy McCullough, who played 268 times and scored 5 goals between 1958 and 1966.

3 Danny Welbeck, who signed from Manchester United in September 2014.

4 George Male, who made 318 appearances between 1930 and 1948, then coached the youth and reserve teams and worked as an Arsenal scout, credited with bringing Charlie George, among others, to the club's attention.

5 Steve Walford, who made 98 Arsenal appearances between 1977 and 1981, scoring 4 goals, and assisted Martin O'Neill at a string of clubs including Wycombe, Leicester, Celtic, Aston Villa and Sunderland.

6 Joe Mercer (FA Cup final captain in 1950 and 1952), and Frank McLintock (FA Cup final captain in 1971 and 1972, and League Cup final captain in 1968 and 1969).

7 Joe Wade (93 appearances between 1946 and 1954, including 40 in the 1952/53 title-winning campaign), and Len Wills (209 appearances and 4 goals, 1953–61).

8 Paul Merson, who scored 99 goals in 425 appearances for Arsenal between 1986 and 1997.

9 Sylvain Wiltord, whose goal in the 1–0 win over
Manchester United at Old Trafford confirmed Arsenal
as champions, and Double-winners, in 2001/02. Wiltord,
who joined Arsenal in 2000 and left in 2004, had won the
French Ligue 1 title with Bordeaux in 1998/99 and then
won it three seasons running with Lyon (2004/05, 2005/06,
2006/07).

10 Johnny MacLeod, who joined Arsenal in July 1961 and
left for Aston Villa on 7 September 1964 – having scored
against the Villans in a 3–1 win at Highbury the previous
weekend.

11 (1) Alex Wilson and Frank Moss. Alex got his break when
Frank suffered a shoulder injury at Everton in 1935 that
sidelined him for virtually the whole of the following season,
one that culminated in Arsenal winning the FA Cup for
the second time, with Wilson between the posts. (2) Bob
Wilson and Ian McKechnie. Schoolteacher Bob joined on
amateur forms from Wolves in summer 1963 and was
handed his Arsenal debut when Ian (who himself had come
into the side for injured first-choice Jack McClelland) was
dropped. Wilson had a run of five games before the arrival
of Jim Furnell, but eventually replaced Furnell as Arsenal's
Number 1 in 1968, and never looked back.

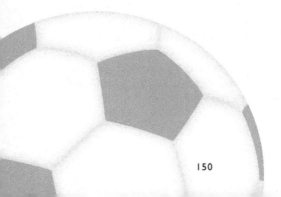

European Adventures

1 Arsenal played 15 European matches during the 1999/2000 season. They played six Champions League group matches but finished third behind Barcelona and Fiorentina, and accordingly dropped into the UEFA Cup, playing 9 matches in that competition including the final against Galatasaray. They played 14 European matches in both 2000/01 and 2008/09, and 13 in 2005/06.

2 After Baker and Strong, the next Gunner to claim a European hat-trick was Alan Smith, who scored 4 against FK Austria Memphis in a European Cup tie at Highbury in September 1991. Then came Ray Parlour (v Werder Bremen, UEFA Cup, March 2000); Thierry Henry (v Roma, Champions League, November 2002); Nicklas Bendtner (v Porto, Champions League, March 2010); Danny Welbeck (v Galatasaray, Champions League, October 2014); and Olivier Giroud (v Olympiakos, Champions League, December 2015).

3 Bayern Munich: Arsenal had played 10 matches against Bayern (winning 3, drawing 2 and losing 5). They'd played 9 against Barcelona (W1 D2 L6), and 8 against each of Ajax, Borussia Dortmund, Olympiakos and Panathinaikos.

4 Besiktas and Galatasaray.

5 Ray Parlour and Lee Dixon.

6 Eduardo.

7 Exactly 200.

8 Germany – the Gunners had played thirty-six games against German opposition (ten different clubs, including both East and West German sides prior to unification). Next in the list are Italy on thirty-three (eleven clubs), Spain thirty-one (nine clubs) and France twenty-five (nine clubs).

9 Colin Pates, Eddie McGoldrick and Ian Selley. Pates scored his goal against Benfica at Highbury in the second leg of a European Champions' Cup 2nd Round tie which the Gunners lost 1–3 after extra-time. McGoldrick spectacularly scored Arsenal's final goal in a 7–0 rout of Standard Liege in Belgium on 3 November 1993, a second round, second leg Cup Winners' Cup tie. Selley had earlier scored in the same match, and the following season at the same stage of the same competition he was also on target when Arsenal hosted Brondby of Denmark, drawing 2–2 on 3 November 1994 to progress 4–3 on aggregate. None of the trio scored for the club again.

10 Ironically, it's against other clubs from England that Arsenal have fared least impressively in European competition. They have failed to win any of their 6 Champions League matches to date against fellow English teams, drawing and losing against both Chelsea and Liverpool, and losing twice against Manchester United. The next most troublesome opponents have been Russian (one win in eight games for a win percentage of 12.75 per cent). At the other end of the spectrum, the Gunners boast 100 per cent records against Bulgarian, Cypriot, Romanian, Scottish and Swiss clubs.

11 Since 16 September 2009, when they beat Standard Liege 3–2 in Belgium after trailing 2–0. The goal-scorers in Liege were Nicklas Bendtner, Thomas Vermaelen and Eduardo; seven years later against Ludogorets in Sofia the Gunners' scorers were Granit Xhaka, Olivier Giroud and Mesut Ozil.

1–0 to the Arsenal

1 Frank Stapleton.
2 1–0 down, 2–1 up. In the semi-final against Spurs, the Gunners, trailing 1–0 from the first leg at Highbury, went 1–0 down at White Hart Lane before scoring twice through Viv Anderson and Niall Quinn to force a third match, also at the Lane. Arsenal again fell behind but Ian Allinson and David Rocastle scored in the last 8 minutes to win 2–1 and secure a Wembley final, in which Ian Rush put Liverpool ahead. But 2 Charlie Nicholas goals gave Arsenal another 2–1 win – and George Graham's side the cup.
3 David Jack.
4 It was the win Arsenal needed – in the last match of the season – to clinch their seventh League title and deny Preston North End their first since 1890. But at 3–2 up with 35 minutes to go and their defence enduring a relentless bombardment, the Gunners knew that a Burnley goal would deny them the championship. They held out and claimed the title on goal average – by a mere 0.099 of a goal.
5 Anders Limpar scored the winner, and was one of the prime targets when a brawl broke out during the match that involved twenty-one players and resulted in the FA subsequently deducting Arsenal 2 points. That left them 8 points behind leaders Liverpool – but the Gunners overhauled the Reds to clinch the 1990/91 title by a 7-point margin, despite the deduction.

6 Danny Welbeck, in his first competitive game for some ten months following injury.

7 Robin van Persie and Andrey Arshavin.

8 Paul Merson, who had also produced an audacious back-heel into Smith's path in the earlier Highbury encounter which the striker gratefully hammered into Liverpool's net.

9 Arsenal won 3–2 after extra-time. Alan Smith put them ahead, Carl Shutt equalised and Gary McAllister gave Leeds a 2–1 lead. With time running out Ian Wright levelled to send the tie into extra-time. And after Paul Merson had hit the post, Wright fired in a shot that just beat former and future Arsenal keeper John Lukic.

10 It was played at Highfield Road, Coventry City's former stadium, and the winning goal was scored by Brian Talbot.

11 (1) O'Leary was making his 622nd appearance for Arsenal, breaking George Armstrong's club record; (2) Dixon's first goal was a penalty – the first he'd taken in the League, and he scored his second by knocking in the rebound after Gunn had saved his second spot-kick; (3) Niall Quinn.

Finals Fling

1 Thirty-three – nineteen FA Cup (1927, 1930, 1932, 1936, 1950, 1952, 1971, 1972, 1978, 1979, 1980, 1993, 1998, 2001, 2002, 2003, 2005, 2014, 2015), 7 League Cup (1968, 1969, 1987, 1988, 1993, 2007, 2011), and seven in Europe (1970 Fairs Cup; 1980, 1994 and 1995 Cup Winner's Cup; 1995 Super Cup; 2000 UEFA Cup; 2006 Champions League).

2 Four – 1950, 1971, 1979 and 2015.

3 Charlie Buchan led out the first Arsenal team to contest an FA Cup final (1927), and Per Mertesacker was skipper in 2015 (club captain Mikel Arteta didn't play any FA Cup matches in 2014/15).

4 Frank McLintock was Arsenal skipper when they met Anderlecht over two legs in the 1970 European Fairs Cup final, while Thierry Henry wore the armband in the 2006 Champions League final against Barcelona.

5 Reg Lewis, Eddie Kelly, Charlie Nicholas, Ian Wright, Alan Smith, Freddie Ljungberg and Theo Walcott all scored 2 cup final goals. Lewis and Nicholas both scored twice in one match, and in each case the opponents were Liverpool, albeit thirty-seven years apart.

6 Terry Neill, who replaced David Jenkins in the 1968 League Cup final against Leeds United.

7 As well as representing Arsenal during their careers, they also played against Arsenal in cup finals: Talbot and Mariner for Ipswich, 1978; Anderson – Sheffield Wednesday, 1993; Gallas and Petit – Chelsea, 2002; Silvestre – Manchester United, 2005; Van Bronckhorst – Barcelona, 2006; Cech and Diarra – Chelsea, 2007; Larsson – Birmingham City, 2011.

8 Fittingly, former club captains David O'Leary (v Sheffield Wednesday in 1993), Tony Adams (v Chelsea in 2002) and Patrick Vieira (v Manchester United in 2005) all bowed out on a high by making their last competitive appearance for the Gunners as part of an FA Cup-winning team. Between them the trio made a combined 1,551 appearances for Arsenal and scored 167 goals.

9 They all scored cup final goals for Arsenal after coming on as substitutes (Kennedy v Anderlecht, 1970; Kelly v Liverpool, 1971; Hayes v Luton Town, 1988; Giroud v Aston Villa, 2015).

10 The four players sent off in cup finals are José Antonio Reyes v Manchester United, 2005; Jens Lehmann v Barcelona, 2006; and Kolo Toure and Emmanuel Adebayor v Chelsea, 2007.

11 Arsenal have come from behind to win four cup finals: in 1971 (FA Cup), 1987 (League Cup), 1993 (League Cup), and 2014 (FA Cup). Give yourself a bonus if you also included the 1970 European Fairs Cup final, in which Arsenal came from 3–1 down in the first leg to triumph 4–3 on aggregate.

End-Game

1 The last home game in Plumstead was played at the Manor Ground on 26 April 1913, with Arsenal and Middlesbrough drawing 1–1. Stephen Stonley scored Arsenal's final League goal at the stadium, in front of a meagre crowd of 3,000.

2 It was a Division 2 game against Nottingham Forest at Highbury on 24 April 1915. Arsenal won 7–0 with 2 goals from Bob Benson, four from Henry King and one from Jock Rutherford. That was the final game of the 1914/15 season, and competitive football was then suspended for the remainder of the First World War. By the time League football resumed in August 1919, Arsenal had been elected to the First Division and have remained in the top tier ever since.

3 It originally showed Birmingham in fifth place and Arsenal in sixth, both having finished on 43 points. But in 1975 it was discovered that an error had been made in 1915 in the calculation of goal average: Arsenal's was in fact superior to Birmingham's. The table was accordingly corrected and Arsenal are now recognised as having finished fifth that season, not sixth.

4 On 2 September 1939, Arsenal played their third match of the embryonic 1939/40 season, beating Sunderland 5–2 at Highbury with four goals from Ted Drake and one from George Drury. The Gunners had drawn 2–2 away to Wolves and beaten Blackburn Rovers 1–0 prior to the visit of Sunderland – but all results were expunged from the record books when League football was abandoned immediately war was declared.

5 Alf Kirchen and Ted Drake.

6 Ian Wright scored (1) his 185th and last Arsenal goal in a 2–1 victory over West Ham United at Upton Park in a League Cup quarter-final on 6 January 1998; exactly one month earlier, on 6 December 1997, Wrighty scored (2) what proved to be his last League goal for Arsenal in a 1–0 win over Newcastle United at St James' Park; and his final Highbury goal had come on 4 October 1997 in a 5–0 defeat of Barnsley.

7 Arsenal beat Sunderland 2–0 at Highbury, with late goals from John Hartson and Ray Parlour, on 28 September 1996. It was the final game of Pat Rice's 4-match tenure as caretaker manager between the departure to QPR of previous caretaker Stewart Houston and the appointment of Arsene Wenger.

8 Scott Marshall scored after 2 minutes of Arsenal's 2–0 victory over Newcastle United in a Premier League game at Highbury on 23 March 1996, while Northern Irishman Stephen Morrow scored Arsenal's goal in a 1–3 defeat against Blackburn Rovers at Ewood Park on 8 March 1995.

9 Thierry Henry scored a hat-trick; Philippe Senderos, Robert Pires, Gilberto Silva and Alexandr Hleb added the other four.

10 They finished twelfth in the Premier League in 1994/95 – George Graham's last season as manager, when Stewart Houston took over on a caretaker basis for the final 14 matches. Thereafter, the lowest Arsenal had finished up to 2015/16 was fifth (in Bruce Rioch's solitary season in charge).

11 That was also in 1994/95, and even in that troubled season, Arsenal still made it to a European final.